AFTER THERMOPYLAE

EMBLEMS OF ANTIQUITY

Font of Life
Ambrose, Augustine, and the Mystery of Baptism
GARRY WILLS

Medusa's Gaze
The Extraordinary Journey of the Tazza Farnese
MARINA BELOZERSKAYA

The Throne of Adulis
Red Sea Wars on the Eve of Islam
G. W. BOWERSOCK

After Thermopylae
The Oath of Plataea and the End of the
Graeco-Persian Wars
PAUL CARTLEDGE

AFTER
THERMOPYLAE

THE OATH OF PLATAEA AND THE END
OF THE GRAECO-PERSIAN WARS

PAUL CARTLEDGE

OXFORD
UNIVERSITY PRESS

OXFORD
UNIVERSITY PRESS

Oxford University Press is a department of the University of Oxford.
It furthers the University's objective of excellence in research,
scholarship, and education by publishing worldwide.

Oxford   New York
Auckland   Cape Town   Dar es Salaam   Hong Kong   Karachi
Kuala Lumpur   Madrid   Melbourne   Mexico City   Nairobi
New Delhi   Shanghai   Taipei   Toronto

With offices in
Argentina   Austria   Brazil   Chile   Czech Republic   France   Greece
Guatemala   Hungary   Italy   Japan   Poland   Portugal   Singapore
South Korea   Switzerland   Thailand   Turkey   Ukraine   Vietnam

Oxford is a registered trade mark of Oxford University Press
in the UK and certain other countries.

Published in the United States of America by
Oxford University Press
198 Madison Avenue, New York, NY 10016

Library of Congress Cataloging-in-Publication Data
Cartledge, Paul.
After Thermopylae : the oath of Plataea and the end of the
Graeco-Persian Wars / Paul Cartledge.
pages cm.—(Emblems of antiquity)
Includes bibliographical references and index.
ISBN 978-0-19-974732-0
1. Plataea, Battle of, Plataiai, Greece, 479 B.C. I. Title.
DF225.7.C37   2013
938'.03—dc23   2013010296

1 3 5 7 9 8 6 4 2

Printed in the United States of America
on acid-free paper

To the memory of John David Lewis (1955–2012)

Contents

———

CONTENTS

viii

Maps and Illustrations

———

The "Persian Wars," as they are widely known, because typically they are looked at from a Greek viewpoint, are famous enough not to need any special attention. The names of Marathon, Thermopylae, and Salamis are as celebrated in their way as those of Hastings, Blenheim, and Waterloo in the annals of English (or British) military history. Indeed, the classically educated Victorian political philosopher and activist John Stuart Mill was once famously moved to claim that Marathon was more important than Hastings, even as an event in *English* history! That claim may seem extraordinary, almost outlandish, but it chimed with his high-Victorian readership's view that the ancient Greeks and especially the ancient Athenians were their cultural ancestors, and that there was at least an imagined continuum between the Greeks' fifth-century BCE culture and that of the English or British in the nineteenth century CE.

But memory of the Persian Wars was also then, as it often still is, highly selective. Will Cinderella—the Battle of Plataea—be allowed to go to this ball? Not always, nor indeed very often. If the ancient Persian empire could quite recently be called—or mislabeled—"the forgotten empire" (in an important exhibition held at the British Museum), how much more deservedly is the epithet "forgotten" to be attached, ironically enough, to the Battle of Plataea, the land battle that actually decided the Persian Wars. Giles MacDonogh's *Great Battles. 50 Key Battles from the Ancient World to the Present Day* (2010) is just one of the most recent such compilations—or rather selections—known to me that manages to include Thermopylae and Salamis but yet to exclude Plataea. Going back three-quarters of a century, we find that Compton Mackenzie's brief but sharp essay of 1934 subtitled *The Battles that Defined the Western World* is significantly and typically entitled *Marathon & Salamis*, not, as of course it should have been, "Marathon, Salamis & Plataea." But at least Mackenzie did have the proper decency to acknowledge in his text that it was Plataea, and not either of his two titular battles, that was "the decisive battle" (p. 136). Sadly, the register of long oblivion could easily be extended back in time, as far indeed as Mill and beyond.

It was therefore with alacrity that I accepted the challenge thrown down to me by the Oxford University Press (New York) to contribute to their new "Emblems of Antiquity" series with a book paying due homage to the Battle of Plataea as a key and pivotal moment not just in ancient or classical Greek history but in all Western history. This book, like the series as a whole, is the brainchild of the ever-inventive Stefan Vranka, and it has been a pleasure as well as a stimulating learning experience to work, again, with him and his colleagues in New York. In accordance with the aims and objectives of the series, this book is addressed to a wide general readership, but yet it has some academic scaffolding and infrastructure too, and through its Epameinondas-like (oblique, slantwise) manner of approach to the battle *via* the Oath of Plataea (rather than more head-on, *via* the so-called Serpent Column victory monument, say) it is hoped that some new or newer light may be shed on the topic in general, and not just for general readers but even perhaps for some of my ancient historian colleagues in the field too.

The position I held from 2006 to 2010 of (visiting) Global Distinguished Professor in the excellent Department of Classics at New York University greatly facilitated the negotiations leading to the contracting of the book. At N.Y.U. I have also to thank most warmly President John Sexton, former Deans Dick Foley and Matthew Santirocco, Associate Dean Jonathan Friedman, and colleagues in the Classics Department—too many to name them all, though I absolutely must name Phillip Mitsis, Joan Connelly, and Mike Peachin. Likewise, various collaborations with the marvelous Director of the NYC-based Onassis Cultural Foundation (USA), Ambassador Loukas Tsilas, and his right-hand woman Amalia Cosmetatou have been both a constant encouragement and a constant reminder that it was a key part of my N.Y.U. Global Distinguished Professorship remit to reach out to the Hellenic community in New York City and environs. For their unstinting *philoxenia* I thank them most warmly. I must also warmly thank the

Press's three anonymous referees, to one of whom I am particularly indebted for imposing a degree of clarity of vision and structure that the text had somehow not hitherto managed to achieve by itself.

Coincidentally, another of my USA publishers is firmly located, like N.Y.U., downtown; many a memorable encounter over breakfast in the Mercer Kitchen with Peter Mayer, owner of the Overlook Press (and former owner of Duckworth-Overlook in the UK), stay happily in the memory. But a further word of thanks must go, not to a US but to a French publishing house, hitherto quite unknown to me: LEMME edit. Just as I was entering the final stages of researching and composing this book, there came to my notice J-N. Corvisier's also brief (101 small pages) but scholarly *La bataille de Platées, 479 av. J-C.* (Corvisier 2011). I could not agree more with the author's first sentence: "The battle of Plataea is one of History's unloved"—a Cinderella, as I've called it myself, something like, say, the World War II battles of Kursk and the Leyte Gulf. Between us two, however, and now also my friend William Shepherd—his quite excellent account of the battle itself (Shepherd 2012) is neatly summarized in his brief article entitled "The most glorious victory ever seen" (*ad fam* vol. XXXII, 2012, 111–12)—I hope we will have done something to dispel for good that misguided perception. William has also very generously cast an eye over a complete draft, as have Dr. Jan Parker and my Cambridge doctoral student Ms. Carol Atack.

To all these I am profoundly grateful, but none of them of course is to be considered implicated in the result, which as noted is aimed, chiefly, at nonspecialist readers with an acute interest in the ancient Greek world and its legacy. This aim has entailed a lighter touch with some of the more detailed argumentation than might otherwise have been expected or demanded. Likewise, rather than encumber the text with footnotes or endnotes, I have offered instead a discursive section of Further Reading suggestions, under the following six headings: I. Primary Sources; II. Secondary Sources; III. The Battle Itself; IV. Religion; V. Commemorations; and, finally, VI. Clash of civilizations? Literature, scholarly and otherwise, referred to for short by author and date (e.g., Shepherd 2012) is listed systematically in the Bibliography.

I dedicate this book, finally, to the memory of my remarkable former PhD student, John David Lewis, who was untimely ripped from us shortly before I completed it. He turned himself into a professional academic classical historian as a very mature PhD student, and in the sadly short time allotted to him thereafter was able to publish no fewer than three very good books, one of which (Lewis 2010) has a first chapter, "'To Look without Flinching': The Greco-Persian Wars, 547–446 BCE," which overlaps with the subject matter of this book and offers a powerful reading of the ideology of Xerxes as a determining factor in the course and outcome of the mighty conflict of 480/79 BCE.

Trumpington,
Cambridge,
July 2012

Map 1. The Aegean Greek World in the Classical Period. From
Cartledge, *Ancient Greece* (2009).

Abdera

Thasos

Samothrace

Imbros

Lemnos

cyros

Byzantium
Chalcedon

Perinthus

Propontis

Cyzicus

Sestus • Lampsacus

Hellespont

Elaeus • Abydus

Sigeum ○ Troy

Tenedos

M Y S I A

P H R Y G I A

Assus • Gargara

Mytilene Pergamum

Eresus

Lesbos

Colcus

Pilane

Cyme ○

Phocaea

L Y D I A

Psara

Hermus

Chios

Chios

Smyrna

Sardis ○

Erythrae

Clazomenae

Teos

Colophon

Lebedus

Cayster

Ephesus ○

I O N I A

Andros

Samos

Samos ○

Maeander

Icaria

Magnesia

Tenos

Myconos

Delos

Miletus

Didyma ○

C A R I A

Paros

Naxos

Myndus

Halicarnassus

hnos

Amorcos

Cos

L Y C I A

Thera

Anaphe

Ialysus

Camirus

Cnidus

Rhodes

Xanthus ○

Rhodes

Lindus

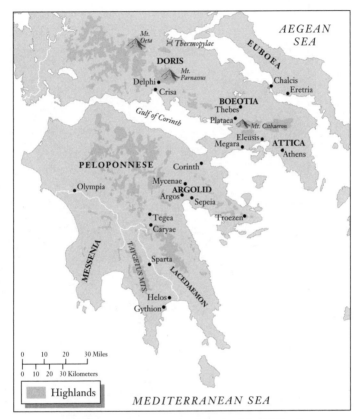

AEGEAN SEA

Mt. Oeta

Thermopylae

EUBOEA

DORIS

Mt. Parnassus

Delphi

Crisa

Chalcis

Eretria

BOEOTIA

Thebes

Gulf of Corinth

Plataea

Mt. Cithaeron

Eleusis

ATTICA

Megara

Athens

PELOPONNESE

Corinth

Olympia

Mycenae

ARGOLID

Argos

Sepeia

Tegea

Troezen

Caryae

MESSENIA

TAYGETUS MTS.

Sparta

LACEDAEMON

Helos

Gythion

0   10   20   30 Miles

0   10   20   30 Kilometers

Highlands

MEDITERRANEAN SEA

Map 2. Central and Southern Mainland Greece. After Holland,
Persian Fire (2007).

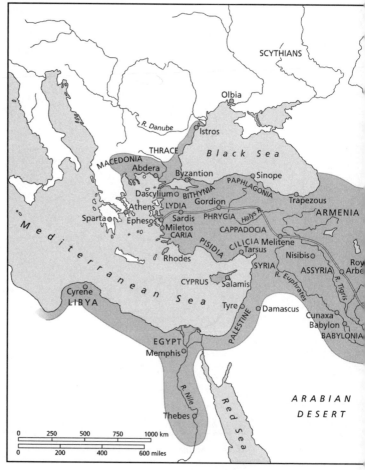

Map 3. The Persian Empire. From Bang and Scheidel, *The Oxford Handbook of the State in the Ancient Near East and Mediterranean* (2013).

Achaemenid Empire about 500 BC
Royal Road

Aral Sea

Caspian Sea

Jaxartes R.

MASSAGETAI

CHORASMIA

Oxus R.

SOGDIANA

Cyropolis

Bactra

MARGIANA

BACTRIA

PARAPANISUS

Taxila

Hecatompylos

ARIA

GANDHARA

Rhagae

DRANGIANA

Ecbatana

MEDIA

PARTHIA

Behistun

ARACHOSIA

Susa

INDIA

SUSIANA

Pasargadae

R. Indus

PERSIS

CARMANIA

Persepolis

GEDROSIA

Persian Gulf

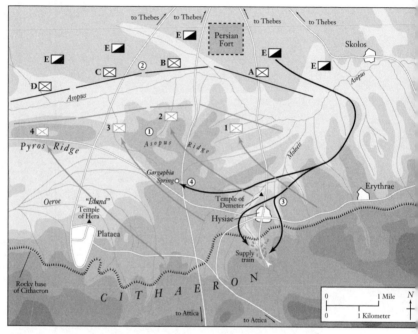

Map 4. Sketch Map of the Plataea Battle, Middle Phase. After Shepherd, *Plataea 479 BC* (2012).

Persian Forces

A Persians, 40,000
B Medes, 20,000
C Bactrians, Indians, and Sacae, 20,000
D Medizing Greeks (hoplites and light-armed), 20,000
E Cavalry (total), 5,000

Greek Forces (hoplites and light-armed)

1 Right: Spartans, Lacedaemonians, Tegeans, Thespians, 20,000
2 Right-Center: Corinthians, Potidaeans, Arcadians of Orchomenus, Sicyonians, 15,000
3 Left-Center: Epidaurians, Troezenians, Lepreans, Mycenaeans and Tirynthians, Phleiasians, Hermionians, Eretrians and Styrians, Chalcidians, Ambraciots, Anactorians and Leucadians, Paleans, Aeginetans, 15,000
4 Left: Megarians, Plataeans, Athenians, 20,000

Timeline

———

All dates down to 508/7 BCE are approximate and/or traditional.

1100 (to 700)   Era of Migrations (Dorian migration, settlement of Asia Minor coast, beginnings of Western colonization, Medes and Persians settle in Iran)

776   Foundation of Olympic Games

750   Greek alphabet invented

700   Poems of Homer, Hesiod

700/650   Introduction of hoplite fighting

600	Thales of Miletus
550	Persian empire founded by Cyrus II ("the Great")
546	Cyrus defeats Croesus King of Lydia, absorbs Greeks of Asia Minor
539	Cyrus takes Babylon, frees Jews
530	Death of Cyrus, succeeded by son Cambyses
525	Cambyses conquers Egypt
522	Death of Cambyses (suicide? murder?); interregnum
521	Darius I assumes throne, reasserts order over empire
510	Hippias tyrant of Athens deposed by Sparta, flees to Persia
508/7	Cleisthenes introduces democratic reforms at Athens; Athens gives earth and water (tokens of submission) to satrap of Lydia at Sardis

505	Sparta's "Peloponnesian League" (modern term) alliance formed
499 (to 494)	Ionian Revolt: rebellion against Persia of Ionian Greeks and other Greek and non-Greek subjects
494	Battle of Lade: final naval defeat of rebellion
490	Battle of Marathon: Athens and Plataea defeat Persian invaders; heroic burial mound at Marathon; victory monument erected at Athens of official commander-in-chief Callicrates
481	Formation of "Hellenic League" (modern term) alliance against Persia
480	Second Persian invasion of mainland Greece, under Xerxes: Battles of Thermopylae and Salamis
480	Battle of Himera: Sicilian Greeks under Gelon defeat Carthaginians
479	**Oath of Plataea** (authenticity disputed). Battles of Plataea and Mycale; "Serpent Column" victory monument of "Greeks" set up at Delphi

478 (to 404)	Athens founds anti-Persian "Delian League" (modern term) alliance
462	Athens: further democratic reforms of Ephialtes and Pericles
460 (to 446/5)	"First" Peloponnesian War: Sparta and allies vs. Athens and allies
449	Peace of Callias (authenticity disputed) between Athens and Persia
447	Parthenon begun, as Persian Wars memorial (completed 432)
446 /5	Thirty Years' Truce between Sparta and Athens (lasted only 14 years)
431 (to 404, with interruption)	Atheno-Peloponnesian War
421(to 414)	Peace of Nicias
404	Sparta, with Persian aid, wins Atheno-Peloponnesian War
404 (to 371)	Spartan hegemony in Aegean Greece

401 (to 400)	Expedition of the "10,000" Greek mercenaries to Asia supported by Sparta; Persian pretender Cyrus the Younger killed in battle at Cunaxa
399	Sparta begins war against Great King Artaxerxes II of Persia
395 (to 386)	Corinthian War: Sparta defeats Quadruple Alliance (Athens, Boeotia, Argos, Corinth), again with Persian aid
386	King's Peace (first "Common Peace"): sponsored jointly by Artaxerxes II of Persia and Agesilaus II of Sparta (known also as Peace of Antalcidas)
378	Athens founds anti-Spartan Second Sea-League
371	Boeotians defeat Sparta at Leuctra
366	End of Sparta's Peloponnesian League
362	(Second) Battle of Mantinea: Boeotians defeat Athens and Sparta; Common Peace renewed
359	Accession of Philip II of Macedon

346	Peace of Philocrates: Philip's hegemony over Athens formally recognized
338	Battle of Chaeronea: Macedon defeats Athens and Thebes; foundation of League of Corinth, Philip chosen commander of "Greeks" versus Persia
336	Murder of Philip II, accession of Alexander III of Macedon (later "the Great")
335	Alexander orders destruction of Thebes
334	Alexander assumes command of invasion of Persian empire
331	Foundation of Alexandria in Egypt (April), Battle of Gaugamela (October)
330	End of Achaemenid Persian empire; sack of Persepolis by Alexander
323	Death of Alexander at Babylon
(CE) **1932**	Discovery of "Oath of Plataea" document
1938	Initial publication of "Oath" document

AFTER THERMOPYLAE

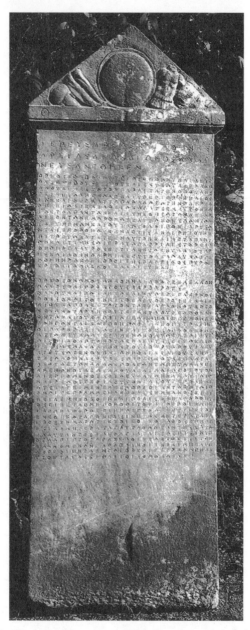

Figure 1.1. The stele of Pentelic marble dedicated at ancient Acharnae by Dion son of Dion the priest of Ares and Athena Areia, bearing images of hoplite equipment above and texts of the Oath of the Ephebes and the Oath of Plataea below. The letters are mostly well cut and (except for lines 1–4) disposed in the stoichedon (grid-pattern) style. Date: third quarter of the 4th century BCE. Found at Menidhi (now renamed Acharnae), 1932. Photo courtesy of the École française d'Athènes.

1

INTRODUCTION

Arms and the Men

Emblems, a word of ancient Greek derivation, have a long history; books of them—such as those of the Renaissance jurist Andrea Alciati (1531)—have enjoyed great currency. Emblems in this sense are pictures containing multiple symbols and allegorical meanings. This book in the "Emblems" series takes as its focus a document from Graeco-Roman antiquity. It contains multiple symbols and is susceptible of yielding meanings of different sorts. I should make it clear, right from the start, where I stand on the issue of just one of those possible meanings: the complicated question of the document's authenticity.

In the literal sense, as a text inscribed upon a finely honed and adorned piece of Athenian marble sometime during the third quarter of the fourth century BCE, the version of the "Oath of Plataea" included here is unarguably authentic—no one has faked the monument as a whole of which the document in question forms a part. The question rather is whether the text that I am primarily concerned with, in form an oath, really was, as it proclaims itself to have been, sworn by Greeks just before the Battle of Plataea in summer 479. To that question after long deliberation I have come firmly to believe that the answer must be in the negative. The arguments for its inauthenticity, in this sense, are set out in some detail later on in the book, in chapter 4. But here I must spell out the following immediate consequence of that judgment: that the text I am primarily discussing here is an emblem, not or not so much of the Graeco-Persian Wars of 480–479 BCE, but rather of fourth-century BCE Athenian culture or more precisely, of Athenian identity and propaganda, since it represents part, a key part indeed, of what the Athenians of the later fourth century BCE wanted to believe and to convince others had been the case in 479. For that in turn, they thought, made a vital difference to how they saw themselves and wanted to be seen by others at that time.

The document in question is illustrated, but it is not itself a picture. Rather, it is what we historians of ancient Greece call rather unhelpfully an "inscription"—a documentary source in contrast to other written evidence that is lumped together under the heading of "literary." Inscriptions vary a great deal in kind and content. They offer the possibility of valuable insights, as well as a particular set of interpretational problems. Study of them began in earnest in the Renaissance, but it was not until the nineteenth century that whole corpora of inscriptions began to be assembled, at first in Germany; and it was in Germany too that they began to be exploited professionally as historical evidence. But their seeming oddity—and often markedly *un*literary character—gave rise to a rather grotesque distinction between inscriptions in general—any texts or pieces of ancient writing on stone, bronze, or some other imperishable material—and "historical" inscriptions in particular, that is, those which had a greater affinity with the sort of subject matter dealt with typically by the ancient "literary" historians from Herodotus and Thucydides onwards. That means war, politics, and diplomacy above all, rather than matters of culture and society (though Herodotus is of course himself a rather major exception to this general ancient trend since he believed that a society's moral or cultural norms might be a crucial historical variable).

Actually, all inscriptions are potentially historical—that is, they all potentially afford subject matter and insight for the historian of the ancient world. They document a very wide range of activities performed by a broad spectrum of people, whether as individuals or as collectivities, in widely varying contexts. All presuppose some form of literacy, but different ancient societies spent more or less time on creating inscriptions. In some societies it is even possible for us to talk of the development of an "epigraphic habit." One such society was that of ancient Athens—or more specifically ancient democratic Athens. For it was a key part of the ideology of people-power (the literal meaning of *dêmo-kratia*) that texts directly affecting the status and conduct of Athenian citizens as citizens of a direct, participatory democracy should ideally be published in semi-permanent or permanent form, and placed conspicuously in spaces of the greatest communal or political significance, such as the city or town square or in the religious space of the high city or *Acro-polis*, to enable any citizen who wished to read them or at least have them read to him.

In our particular case, in this book, we are dealing with a fascinating epigraphic (inscriptional) document, which is not self-standing but forms part of a larger, composite epigraphic monument. The whole epigraphic text—a preamble followed by 51 lines—was inscribed at some point between 350 and 325 BCE on a pedimental stele (a pillar with gable topping) made of local Attic marble. The stele was originally erected in the countryside of Attica (the territory of Athens) at a religious shrine within the settlement of Acharnae, which was one of the 139 or 140 demes (villages, parishes, wards) constituting the *polis* (state, city, or citizen-state) of the Athenians, which at that time enjoyed a political governmental regime of *dêmokratia*, "people-power." The stele was found in the modern village of Menidhi and is now housed in the collection of the French Archaeological School in Athens, the premises of which it entered in 1938 thanks to the good offices of the world-class epigraphist Louis Robert.

After the preamble and a separate document usually referred to as "The Oath of the Ephebes" (which occupies lines 1–20), lines 21–46 constitute what is conventionally referred to as "The Oath of Plataea." The final lines, 46–51, detail the sanctions to be visited upon any violators of the Oath. For-mally speaking, our document is part of a religious offering or dedication made on the community's behalf to Ares, god of War, by his chief priest at Acharnae, Dion son of Dion. This is in itself quite noteworthy. Despite his prominence in the fic-tional world of Homer's *Iliad*, the foundational text of all ancient Greek culture, Ares was conspicuous in the real ancient Greek world by the very scarcity of cult-places or sanctuary-sites, let alone temples, that were consecrated specially to him. His cult-site and temple at Acharnae in Attica (see Map 2) thus stand out in high relief. In terms of its genre, the Oath of Plataea is a religious manifestation. It was sworn in the name of the "gods" (so addressed), which category included god-desses, and reinforced by a following curse invoking those same god(desse)s who would punish the transgressors hor-ribly if the terms of what the Oath prescribed should in any way be breached (see further chapter 3). The text will be fur-ther examined both for its own sake and on its own terms, as an epigraphic document, in chapter 2.

Dion and those of his fellow citizens and worshippers of Acharnae who had the document inscribed, rather lavishly, in the third quarter of the fourth century BCE believed—or wanted viewers and readers to believe—that the Plataea Oath was authentic. That is to say, it was represented to and by them as a literally faithful transcription of a genuine text or docu-ment originating from the Graeco-Persian Wars, that is, some 150 years or five to six generations earlier (chapter 4). More precisely, its alleged historical moment of enactment fell quite soon before the Battle of Plataea, which took place in the summer (end of August or September) of 479 BCE and marked the final defeat of the Persian Empire's attempt to conquer mainland Greece (chapter 5). However, as remarked in the Preface, Plataea is one of those battles in military history that have been unjustly forgotten to a greater or lesser extent. But its neglect is especially ironic, since it was the Greeks' victory here that brought to a conclusion a major war, a true clash of civilizations, between certain Greeks and the Persian empire. It was after this battle that the Greeks dedicated their would-be comprehensive and final victory monument and memorial to the entire war—the accompanying text begins "these [Greek cities and peoples] fought the war." The dedicatee was Apollo, the god of oracular prophecy at Delphi, the navel of the earth, in central Greece (on this so-called Serpent Column, of which precious little remains at Delphi itself, see further chapter 6). Plataea, in short, was one of those historic rarities, a truly decisive battle. Moreover, its result brought a surprisingly positive outcome not just for the Greeks but arguably for the entire future of western civilization as a whole (chapter 7).

In August or September 479 the small town of Plataea, located just south of the always much more important—and usually deeply hostile—city of Thebes, witnessed a massive land battle involving tens of thousands of combatants on each side. This was indeed the largest number of Greeks ever brought together in a common cause pitted against a significantly larger, Persian-led force that also included a distressingly large number of Greeks. It was the Spartans who provided the largest single contingent of the unified Greek forces, together with the overall command and leadership structure; for them, the victory was triumphant vengeance for their heroic but wholesale defeat at Thermopylae the previous year—and reparation, too, for their failure to appear in time for the mainly Athenian victory at Marathon. But what exactly happened on the plain of Plataea? And why has this Spartan victory been relatively overlooked by history? We shall attempt an answer to the first of those questions in chapter 5. Part of the answer to the second can be found in a little-known Oath, our Oath of Plataea, that was purportedly sworn by the leaders of several Greek city-states prior to the battle (chapter 2). The Oath is in form a religious document (chapter 3). Texts of it survive in several versions from the fourth century BCE and later periods; and their very creation and survival tell us much about the early Greek mythology of the Persian Wars, and how the Greeks thought about memorializing these events for posterity (chapter 6).

For to say that "the Greeks" beat the Persians and their allies or subjects in 480–479 BCE is to be rather grossly economical with the truth, or at least downright misleading. In fact, although more than thirty Greek cities fought side by side against the invading Persians, a good number of those cities or peoples who could have joined in on the loyalist side chose not to, either by attempting to remain neutral or by actively joining with the Persian invaders; and even those few that did manage in the end to band together long enough to defeat the invaders did not always agree either about the meaning of these events or about how they should be commemorated. As was the case with much ancient Greek history, the Athenians and Spartans were the chief competitors for control of this slice of the past.

And, judging from the fact that the mainly Athenian victories at Marathon (490) and Salamis (480) have overshadowed to the point of oblivion the essentially Spartan victory at Plataea, we may fairly claim that it was Athens that won this propaganda war—as indeed most others besides. The Oath of Plataea thus both vividly illuminates Greek anxieties over historical memory and reflects the Atheno-Spartan rivalry that erupted in little under fifty years after the Battle of Plataea—in what we usually refer to as the Peloponnesian War (431–404 BCE). Indeed, hostilities actually commenced by proxy at Plataea itself, where (in the words of the War's great historian, Thucydides of Athens) a treaty sworn between Athens and Sparta and their respective allies in 445 BCE and ostensibly destined to last for thirty years "had overtly been broken" by an invasion of Plataea launched by the Thebans in spring 431.

The Oath also provides us with a golden opportunity to discuss anew a host of interesting subjects. These include the Oath's contested and indeed highly dubious authenticity; its reception in Greek antiquity, that is, the references to it and uses made of it by subsequent classical and post-classical individuals and cultures; the precise, on-the-ground nature of the Greeks' military victory over the Persian invaders; the fraught symbolic issue of what counted as a Greek identity vis-à-vis the "barbarism" of the Persians; the nature of religion in ancient Greece and its role in ancient Greek politics; and, last but not least, the meaning or meanings that the Plataea conflict may still bear for us, as we look back over two-and-a-half millennia (AD 2011 was the 2500th anniversary of the Marathon battle, the 2500th of Plataea will fall in 2022) and reflect upon both our Hellenic inheritance and the appropriate ways to commemorate the victors and victims of warfare—a mode of human interaction that is still all too endemic and apparently considered indispensable. Put differently, I shall be exploring the Oath's significance in the following main manifestations: as a possible source for part of "what actually happened" immediately before and during the Battle of Plataea; as an artifact of Greek, specifically Athenian, mentality and culture in the mid-fourth century BCE—which can be further broken down into, on one hand, what mid-fourth-century Athenians believed or wanted to believe their ancestors and other loyalist (anti-Persian, pro-Hellenic) Greeks really had thought and done in the summer of 479, at a climactic moment in the history of classical Greece as a whole and in the history of Athenian democratic politics and culture in particular, and, on the other, what mid-to-late fourth-century Athenians' contemporary cultural preoccupations and anxieties were; and finally, but not least, as an artifact of ancient Athenian religion, a very different one from any of those with which most of us will be at all intimately familiar.

In short, *After Thermopylae* will aim both to provide a deeply contextualized history of the crucially important but too often neglected Battle of Plataea and to offer a rich portrait of the ancient Greeks' cultural ethos during one of the most critical periods in all ancient (not just ancient Greek) history and its subsequent reception.

2

—————

THE OATH OF PLATAEA

Texts and Contexts

INTRODUCTION

In the early 1930s a farmer working the land in the Attic (Athenian) countryside struck, not gold as he'd doubtless hoped, but a large lump of worked stone. The lump turned out to be an ancient monument, a rather handsomely worked stele (pillar) of local marble, which was both inscribed with texts and decorated in bas relief. It had originally been set up in the ancient village of Acharnae in the foothills of Mount Parnes several kilometers north of the city of Athens. The attention of a leading French epigraphist (specialist in reading and deciphering such texts) was soon drawn to it, which led to its purchase by the French School of Archaeology at Athens (in whose fine premises it still resides).

It's the aim of this chapter to give a close reading of the emblematic text that has come to be known for short as "the Oath of Plataea." We shall first unpack the epigraphic text's literal and associated meanings. Then we shall compare and contrast this inscribed text with two other extant, "literary" versions of the Oath. Both of these are later in date of preservation, one much later. The earlier is contained in a speech delivered by the then preeminent Athenian statesman Lycurgus, in the wake of Athens's stunning defeat by the kingdom of Macedon at the Battle of Chaeronea in central Greece (338 BCE). The later version is to be found in the oddly named *Library of History* (book 11, chapter 29, sections 2–3) compiled in the late-Hellenistic period (first century BCE) by the Sicilian Greek universal historian Diodorus.

This chapter will also talk more about the specific political milieu that originally housed the stele, the deme of Acharnae. "Deme" is the usual anglicization of the ancient Greek word *dêmos*, a protean word that could mean according to context "people," "masses" (or majority)—and village, in the technical sense of parish or ward, a voting district. In that last, technical sense, Attic demes played a cardinal role within the Athenian democratic state as a whole. We shall next address the "authenticity question": that is, try to decide what factual relation if any the epigraphic Oath text bears to the putative original oath, which had allegedly been sworn by Athenians at some time shortly before the Battle of Plataea in 479. Finally, a suggestion will tentatively be made as to why the monument as a whole—comprising the figurally embellished stele, two oath texts, and a supporting curse text—was produced and inscribed. In other words, when, where, how, and by whom it was erected: what, in short, is or are the proper *context* or *contexts* within which it should be read—literally as well as metaphorically—by us?

To anticipate a little further, in the chapter following this the text's religious significance will be more particularly assayed. The ancient Greeks had an extraordinarily rich and plastic vocabulary, but, rather oddly to us at first sight, they did not "have a word for" what we call "religion." That, however, is partly and importantly because for them religion was everywhere; everything was, as one early Greek sage (Thales of Miletus, *floruit* c. 600 BCE) is said to have remarked, "full of gods" (gods—and goddesses—in the plural, because the Greeks were determined polytheists *avant la lettre*). The religious significance of our text is in fact such that it demands its own separate treatment, which will include a discussion of the specific nature of the two principal Olympian Gods invoked right at the start of the entire document by the proudly self-proclaimed dedicant of the stele as a whole, by name Dion son of the homonymous (and perhaps not especially imaginative) Dion.

TEXTS

Gods

> (lines 1–4) The priest of Ares and Athena Areia, Dion son of Dion of [the deme] Acharnae, has dedicated this. [space]

(5) Ancestral oath of ephebes, which the ephebes must swear. I will not shame the sacred arms and armor nor will I desert the man beside me in the line, wherever I shall be stationed. (8) I will defend on behalf of both sacred and profane things, and I will not hand on the fatherland diminished but greater and better so far as in me lies and together with absolutely all. (11) And I will hearken to whoever is wielding power sensibly and will obey both the currently established ordinances and those that may sensibly be established for the future. (14) But if anyone overthrows these, I will not submit to them both so far as in me lies and together with all, and I will honor the ancestral sacred customs. (16) Witnesses the gods and goddesses Aglaurus, Hestia, Enyo, Enyalius, Ares and Athena Areia, Zeus, Thallo, Auxo, Hegemone, Heracles, boundaries of the fatherland, wheat crops, barley crops, vines, olives, figs. [space]

(21) Oath which the Athenians swore when they were about to do battle against the barbarians. [space] I shall fight as long as I am alive, and I shall not value living above my being free. And I shall not desert the Taxiarch or Enomotarch, neither when he is alive nor when dead. And I shall not quit the field unless the commanders lead me away, and I shall do whatsoever the generals order. (29) And I shall bury in the same spot the dead of those who have fought as my allies, and shall leave behind none of them unburied. After winning victory over the barbarians

in battle, I shall tithe the city of the Thebans; (33) and I shall not destroy Athens or Sparta or Plataea or any of the cities which have fought as our allies, nor shall I tolerate their being starved, nor shall I cut them off from running water, whether they be friends or at war. (39) And if I steadfastly observe the oath, as it has been written, may my city be without disease; but if not, may it be sick; and may my city be unravaged; but if not, may it be ravaged; (42) and may it give increase; but if not, may it be barren; and may the women give birth to children like their genitors; but if not, monsters; and may the cattle give birth after their kind; but if not, monsters.

(46–51) These they swore, covering the sacrificial victims with their shields, and to the accompaniment of a trumpet they pronounced a curse: if they were to transgress any part of what had been sworn and were not to observe steadfastly the oath, as it had been written, pollution should be upon those very persons who had sworn. [space]

COMMENTARY

"These" they swore (line 46)—"these" in the plural, because the stele contains texts of not one but two Oaths (*horkoi*), the first, occupying lines 1–20, being the Ephebic Oath (of which there are two later literary versions preserved, indicating, as in the case of the Plataea Oath, its perceived significance both for its own day and for Athenian and Greek memorialization and memory). The relevance of this conjunction of Oaths will be explored more fully later.

Line 21 specifies that the Plataea Oath was sworn by the Athenians, but that probably does not mean to exclude the other members of the Hellenic anti-Persian alliance led by Sparta, "the Hellenes" (as they seem to have called themselves), and in particular Sparta itself, as we shall see in chapter 4. They are said to have sworn it "when they were about to do battle against the barbarians." That need not mean when they were immediately on the point of joining battle; oath-rituals could take some time to perform. Rather, *if* it ever really was sworn, in whatever precise verbal form, then I agree with the majority of commentators who would locate the swearing of it at some point in time and space after the forces led by Sparta, who were coming up north from the Peloponnese, had linked with the forces of Athens and other central Greek cities at Eleusis, before they then advanced conjointly into Boeotia. The battle-cry-of-freedom clause "I shall fight as long as I am alive, and I shall not value living above my being free" is both a ringing ideological declaration of the loyalist Greeks' overarching war aim and a clear echo of the spirit in which the Spartans under Leonidas had—unlike the majority of their allies (the signal exception being the Thespians, who if anything made a greater self-sacrifice even than the Spartans)—stood their ground until death the summer before, in 480 BCE, in the pass at Thermopylae. For the record, the Athenians had had no troops at Thermopylae; their practical contribution to the Hellenic war effort in that first year of resistance was exclusively maritime.

The next two clauses are self-denying prohibitions: "And I shall not desert the taxiarch or enomotarch, neither when he is alive nor when dead." "And I shall not quit the field unless the commanders lead me away, and I shall do whatsoever the generals order." The problem with these clauses from the standpoint of historicity is not only or so much that they mix different levels of command. A "general" (here *hêgemôn*, literally "leader") was a nontechnical term for the highest type of officer, including therefore the commander-in-chief. A taxiarch was a regimental commander, one rung only below that of commander-in-chief, whereas an enomotarch was a far more lowly officer, commander of a mere platoon. The problem, rather, is that the first clause mixes officer titles of two very different Greek military organizations. Thus taxiarchs are certainly Athenian, but enomotarchs are—or seem exclusively to be—Spartan. Before going any further, I should in fairness add here that "taxiarch" was not what was read on the stone by the document's original publisher, Louis Robert, in 1938; it is the corrected reading of Georges Daux, 1965, and surely right. This is a useful reminder that historical problems can be caused by the—frequently encountered—circumstance that the surface of an inscribed document has been damaged, whether in antiquity or much more recently, by a ploughshare, for example. (However, this particular stone is actually quite well preserved.) Yet the loyalist Greeks at Plataea fought in their city units and would not ordinarily expect to have to obey officers supplied by another city's force.

This is one of the inscribed Oath's features that has led a leading scholar (van Wees 2006) to argue that the Oath is really in its ultimate origins not an Athenian but a Spartan text, an "oath taken by Sparta's sworn bands" (131)—by which he means an oath sworn, not exceptionally or uniquely at Plataea or on any other foreign battlefield, but regularly and normally at home in Sparta for purely domestic consumption, and then imposed in this case ad hoc on all its allies at Plataea. That contention seems to me, however, to involve taking an acute perception about one detail of the Oath's wording and spinning it out into an unacceptably broad general claim about the nature of the Oath as a whole. Suppose, for the sake of argument, that this were to have been a text inscribed in Sparta or for Spartans rather than at Acharnae for Athenians, would the Spartans have placed the Athenian taxiarch before the Spartan enomotarch in order of precedence? If that sort of tampering or rearrangement at least be allowed, then the door is open for an interpretation that allows for far more Athenian manipulation—which is indeed, I shall argue, the case of the Oath as a whole.

The second of those negative clauses—especially "I shall do whatsoever the generals order"—poses a problem of a different order. On one hand, the Spartans were themselves famed for their obedience to authority: the quality known in Greek as *peitharkhia*. Yet, on the other hand, if we are to believe Herodotus (see chapter 5), a Spartan commander at Plataea named Amompharetus—whose rank and seniority are not entirely clear—saw fit to disobey no lesser personages than the overall commander-in-chief of the entire loyalist Greek army, his own Spartan regent Pausanias, and his royal deputy. Perhaps the point of the Oath text here is to draw attention, for an

Athenian audience, precisely to that one known and conspicuously odd, out-of-national-character Spartan act? But that may well be thought hypercritical and hyper-suspicious. Moving on . . .

"And I shall bury in the same spot the dead of those who have fought as my allies, and shall leave behind none of them unburied." Rituals of burial were vitally important to all Greeks at all times and in all circumstances. When Herodotus wanted to illustrate extreme differences of cultural norms between different peoples (in this case Greeks and an Indian people), he selected their radically opposed burial customs (book 3, chapter 38). Failure to provide due burial to a kinsman could result, it was generally believed, in serious damage to the living inflicted by the dead person's deeply offended spiritual avatars. Failure to provide or refusal to allow due post-battle burial, as the Thebans insisted upon in the case of the Athenian corpses after the battle of Delium in 424 BCE, was an extreme instance of highly unusual and irregular flouting of this general religious taboo. It is this same concern for proper burial that explains, for example, the utter ferocity with which the Spartans fought at Thermopylae to recover the corpse of Leonidas—to no avail, ultimately; though whether one believes that the Persians really did mutilate it, as Herodotus vividly describes, depends on whether one attributes the no doubt sincere Spartan belief in and report of that alleged decapitation to mere cultural prejudice.

In practice, in Greek summer conditions and in the absence of mummification, burial—whether by inhumation or by cremation—had to take place as soon as possible postmortem.

At any rate by the 460s BCE, it was the Athenians' normal practice to cremate on the spot their dead warriors who died abroad and to bring their ashes home from the battlefield for public ceremonial interment in Athens's major civic cemetery, that located in the city's Potters' Quarter (the Kerameikos). How early that ritual practice goes back is, however, unknown, so we cannot say for certain how exceptional or unexceptional was the Athenians' treatment of the 192 dead fighters of Marathon in 490. These magnificent Few were buried, possibly after cremation, under a huge funerary and memorial mound that was erected on or near the battle site and still to this day survives, like the plain itself, in notably altered form (it has been excavated over the years both scientifically and very much unscientifically). At this holy mound the battle dead were worshipped in after times as heroes (demigods, one rung only below the gods themselves). Spartans, on the other hand, one assumes were regularly buried—like most Greeks and for the obvious reasons—where they died fighting on foreign soil. There is just one, admittedly massive, type of exception to that rule on the record. That is, if a king died abroad in battle or for any other reason, and if his corpse could be recovered, he was first mummified in either wax or honey and then brought home to Sparta for the conduct of an elaborate, dayslong funerary ritual that involved the entire population (unfree as well as free, citizen and noncitizen) and the extensive territory of the Spartan state in Laconia and Messenia.

Next, "After winning victory over the barbarians in battle, I shall tithe the city of the Thebans; and I shall not destroy Athens or Sparta or Plataea or any of the cities which have fought as our allies." "Tithing" in such a context was literal: it referred to the dedication to a god, often Apollo of Delphi, of more or less exactly a tenth part of the value realized by selling the booty seized from a defeated enemy. Or, in the case of a defeated city as here, it meant more metaphorically dedicating an appropriate portion of the sum raised by selling booty extracted from a city that had first been utterly destroyed. An early example of this uncomfortable Greek practice of city-annihilation is afforded by the fate of the—presumably small—city of Arisba on the island of Lesbos. Once there had been six independent cities on that eastern Aegean island, but by Herodotus' day there were only five, and Arisba was no more, having been eliminated by the other five. As it turned out in historical fact after the Plataea victory, the victorious allies did attack "medizing" (i.e., pro-Persian) Thebes, but they did not destroy it utterly. This is the only clause of the epigraphic version of the Oath that was certainly falsified in subsequent practice on the part of its putative swearers. That circumstance could be—but need not be—taken as an argument for the authenticity of at least this clause, since it might be thought odd to invent retrospectively a clause that was not put into practice. On the other hand, it is hard to find historical justification, in the supposed pre-Plataea context, for singling out just Thebes as the one city to be "tithed." Herodotus, who does not mention a pre-Plataea oath, does mention an earlier oath (7.132), supposedly sworn the previous year before Thermopylae, and this more believably contains a general threat to tithe all cities that voluntarily took the Persians' side.

Thebes, somewhat ironically, turned out to be a Greek city-destroyer itself, both indirectly and directly, on several occasions. On the first, in 427, when it was Sparta that did the deed at Thebes' imploring, and then again in 373, when Thebes managed it by and for itself, the victim city was none other than Plataea. (Plataea's crime in Theban eyes was that, though it was ethnically a Boeotian town, it preferred alliance with non-Boeotian Athens to active membership of the Boeotian federal state—dominated by Thebes. In 364 Thebes took its domination to what it considered a logical conclusion—by destroying its main Boeotian rival city, Orchomenus.) That may indeed account for the next sentence of the Oath, which is very oddly phrased indeed: "and I shall not destroy Athens or Sparta or Plataea or any of the cities which have fought as our allies." In 479, and immediately after, surely it would hardly have been necessary to include such a prohibition as that, since it would not have easily been even contemplated or envisaged at that time. On the other hand, in 373, as mentioned, Plataea was actually destroyed by Thebes, as it had been in 426 by Sparta at Thebes' vehement urging.

Nor is that, by any means, the end of this story of inter-Greek violent reprisal and destruction. In 404 Athens, the loser in the Peloponnesian War, was seriously threatened with extinction by the allies of Sparta, led by Thebes, which had profited from the War greatly, and not least at the expense of its near neighbor Athens. So it was a reversal of fortune (what the Greeks called a *peripeteia*) that all too many ancient Greeks would have relished when in 335 Thebes was itself eventually annihilated, if only temporarily—at the behest of Greece's conqueror, Alexander the Great. How could he have justified such a drastic measure? Such was the continuing potency of the miasma of contumely enshrouding Thebes thanks to its blatant policy of medism in 480–479 BCE that it could be invoked in partial justification almost 150 years later by Alexander, acting in his capacity as titular leader of a Panhellenic Greek alliance, though his was surely a symbolic act of severely mundane pragmatism rather than lofty idealism.

There follow further self-imposed prohibitions: "nor shall I tolerate their being starved, nor shall I cut them off from running water, whether they be friends or at war." And finally there comes a self-imposed binding declaration to the effect that, if the swearers do not uphold all the Oath's provisions, they will be deprived therefore of the blessings of freedom from disease, inviolability from enemy attack, and of normal human and animal fertility that strict observance of all the clauses would ensure. The last six lines finally rehearse the sacrificial ritual that was allegedly practiced at the time of the swearing, heavy as it is with the hoplite military symbolism of protection by shields and the blowing of a trumpet. But more important even than that ritual is the self-imposed curse (*ara*) with which the text concludes: transgression of any part of the Oath, it is spelled out, will inevitably envelope the perjurers in religious pollution (the term used here is *agos*, an equivalent of the more usual *miasma*: see further chapter 3). It has often been noted that both the undertaking not to tamper with an enemy's water supply and the curse that supports the Oath overall echo the formulae observed by members of the Amphictyonic League which controlled the sacred site of Delphi; they are cited as such, for example, in a speech of the Athenian orator Aeschines from the mid-340s BCE, which may—or may not—have a bearing on the date and circumstances of production of this epigraphic text of the Plataea Oath.

Before we leave it, one last question regarding precisely its epigraphic, written nature remains: what are we to make of the clause "And if I steadfastly observe the oath, as it has been written . . ." (39–40)? Is this a reference only to this particular written text—or is it (also) to some earlier written text or texts? It seems unlikely to me, at any rate, to be a reference to the alleged aboriginal oath sworn actually before the Battle of Plataea, at Eleusis or wherever, since there wouldn't have been the time or probably the material available for anyone to write it down. Besides, there wouldn't have been felt quite the same need as there would be perhaps by us: Greeks of necessity in a largely oral world of communication had much better developed memories than we do. All the same, the resulting scope for textual or verbal manipulation, for selective memorialization, was there from the very beginning of the process—and was, I suggest, suitably and sufficiently large to be exploited unscrupulously in the interests of a major Greek city whose hoplite warriors had not perhaps achieved on the actual battlefield of Plataea quite as much as their heirs and descendants would ideally have wished for the purposes of the ongoing inter-Greek battles of competitive commemoration. I return to that issue below, especially in chapter 6.

Besides the epigraphic text, there are, as noted at the start of the chapter, two extant literary versions of the Oath, one belonging to the late 330s, the other to the later first century BCE. These two are quite similar to each other but also quite divergent from the epigraphic text (more divergent indeed than the—also two—literary versions of the Ephebic Oath are from the epigraphic version on the Acharnae stele). Moreover, the later of the two sources, Diodorus of Sicily, who is probably quoting here as usual from his own main source, the mid-fourth-century general historian Ephorus of Cyme, locates the swearing of the supposed oath at the Isthmus of Corinth, where delegates of the Hellenic League alliance met for the last time in spring 480, a very long time before the Battle of Plataea specifically. That, combined with the fact that the only oath mentioned by our far and away best source for the Graeco-Persian Wars, Herodotus, is related not to Plataea in 479 but to Thermopylae in 480, is surely enough to dismiss Diodorus-Ephorus' alleged oath from the reckoning as a potentially historical act, regardless of its precise alleged contents. The mention by the Athenian orator Lycurgus, however, although it is nearly contemporary with the epigraphic Oath, only makes his version's divergence from it in detailed content all the more significant and problematic: either we accept the epigraphic version as an authentic document, or we accept Lycurgus's version—or we accept neither.

Here, to begin with, is briefly the context of Lycurgus's version. Quite soon after the Oath was inscribed and dedicated at Acharnae, within twenty years at the outside (I shall suggest below a very much shorter timespan), leading Athenian statesman and politician Lycurgus delivered a prosecution speech against his fellow Athenian Leocrates. The capital charge he brought alleged desertion by Leocrates at the disastrous battle of Chaeronea of 338, in which Athens together with its then major ally Thebes had gone down to total defeat at the hands of Philip II of Macedon, his son Alexander (the future Alexander III "the Great"), and his Greek subject-allies. The prosecution was originally intended for 336 but did not actually materialize until 330, by when Macedon's grip on Greece and Athens was proving unshakeable. Lycurgus, ever the pragmatist, was performing a balancing act. He both wished to raise Athens' morale by referring back to its glory days of successful resistance to a power, the empire of Persia, that was often represented in Athens as even more culturally alien and threatening than Macedon, and at the same time did not wish to advocate the outright rebellion against Macedon that Sparta had unwisely ventured in 331—and from which Athens had stayed conspicuously aloof.

In Lycurgus's literary version the threat to destroy medizing Greek cities is made into a general provision—it is not restricted to the city of Thebes, as in the inscribed Oath. Likewise, the promise not to uproot loyal cities is again made general, not confined to named cities, and is, moreover, placed before instead of after the tithing clause. Rather than the taxiarch (Athenian) and the enomotarch (Spartan) of the inscribed Oath, both literary versions refer more vaguely and generically to "leaders." Those divergences could perhaps be put down to the purely formal linguistic exigencies of literary *versus* epigraphic framing. But I should want to add in to the mix a keen desire on Lycurgus' part not to antagonize Thebes— or rather the scattered remaining Theban citizens, since their city had as we have noted been destroyed on Alexander's orders in 335. However, yet more significant and striking than those verbal differences in shared clauses is the fact that both the literary versions add a clause which constrains the oath-takers from rebuilding the sacred buildings destroyed by the "barbarians" (Persians) and binds them to leave the ruins to stand as a permanent memorial. Since this clause was controverted in practice, admittedly after a considerable interval of time—many of the destroyed Athenian temples were in fact in some sense rebuilt, or, most famously in the case of the Parthenon, reinvented, if over a lengthy period—it has a particular reference and relevance to the authenticity debate. Conversely, both the literary versions omit the curse which, by spelling out that pollution will fall upon any transgressors of any of its clauses, supports the epigraphic Oath. The latter "editing out" renders the literary versions formally inauthentic in this key religious regard at the least.

AUTHENTICITY

So, does the Acharnae stele reproduce a text that is a substantially accurate transmission of an oath originally formulated and sworn in the summer of 479? Argument will continue to ebb and flow both pro and con. There may—in some moods I'm inclined to believe that there must—have been some sort of oath binding together (or papering over the cracks between) the wavering allies of the Hellenic-loyalist anti-Persian alliance sworn either in 481 or at latest spring 480. Indeed, insofar as there was a formal, quasi-legally instituted "Hellenic league," as modern scholars are fond of calling an alliance that the allies may themselves have referred to simply as "the Hellenes," that would indeed have been constituted precisely by the religiously binding mutual oath(s) sworn by the allies—first at the Isthmus of Corinth in early summer 481, and then again at the same venue, sacred to Poseidon, a year or so later. But would that oath or those oaths have been sufficient to harness, guide, and guarantee cooperation between them for the rest of "the war" against the Persians? The one collective Hellenic oath that *is* mentioned by Herodotus (7.132), one that was allegedly sworn not before Plataea but before Thermopylae in summer 480, suggests not. So in principle, since even after the tremendous victory by sea at Salamis the alliance showed large and growing fissures, it's not at all implausible to me that there should have been felt the need for more sealant to be applied, in the shape of a new or renewed oath. And this latter could well have been sworn, conveniently and opportunely enough, at the marshalling ground of Eleusis—another sacred and Panhellenic site—immediately prior to the joint advance northwards to confront Mardonius and his Persian forces in Boeotia. And Eleusis, though the Mysteries celebrated there were Panhellenic, lay on the soil of Attica, politically within the bounds of the citizen-state of Athens. Athenians would thus have had a special reason to want to remember the swearing of an oath precisely there.

However, it is an almost entirely different matter to decide whether the terms of the alleged oath as recorded on the stone at Acharnae and as reported divergently in the literary sources do in any particular accurately reflect the terms of such an oath as may originally—putatively—have been sworn. On that latter point, I remain adamantly sceptical. Overall, I believe that the weight of argument firmly tips the balance in the direction of literal, verbal inauthenticity. And yet in a crucial way that is beside the point, the main point of this book, which is to try to identify and to explain the function(s) the Oath of Plataea was designed to serve in its immediate monumental context.

Those functional needs, I suggest, are to be located firmly within a retrospectively triumphalist narrative—or rather story, in the sense of a fabrication—that the Athenians had begun insistently to tell themselves and anyone else who would listen to them from the mid-380s BCE onwards. A story which acquired a new salience and urgency in the desperate times immediately following the Athenians' calamitous defeat at Chaeronea in 338. Those, I further suggest, are respectively the true overall context and the true specific context within which the monument as a whole is to be properly and fully understood.

CONTEXTS

To return to the momentous events of 480–479 BCE, the "Greek" victory over the Persian invaders in those years had depended crucially on the cooperation of Sparta and Athens. But no sooner had that victory been won than the natural and habitual inclinations of these two radically different political communities had leapt to the fore. In winter 478/7, on the sacred Aegean island of Delos, Athens swore separately from Sparta new binding oaths that inaugurated a new, anti-Persian alliance, one which very soon (Thucydides believed within less than decade) became transformed into an Athenian empire. That naval empire partly necessarily, partly avoidably, was from the very start set on a collision course not only with its ostensible object, the mighty Persian empire, but also with Sparta and its mainly Peloponnesian, mainly land-based alliance. A desultory series of clashes between Athens and Sparta and their respective allies between 460 and 445 was concluded with a supposedly thirty-year truce, but which in practice lasted only fourteen and gave way to a full-blown ancient Greek equivalent of a "world war."

This Atheno-Peloponnesian War lasted on and off for twenty-seven years, a full generation, and ranged all over the Aegean, up into the Hellespont (Dardanelles), and as far west as Sicily. The first phase of the War lasted for a full decade and was rounded off with a peace conventionally named after its chief Athenian negotiator, Nicias. Since the Spartans had started the War with the express aim of terminating the Athenian empire, and since it had failed by a long way to achieve this goal, the peace represented a win on points for Athens. Conversely, when the War resumed in 413, the Athenians, who had restarted it, were in very bad shape militarily after a major defeat in Sicily, and soon in very bad shape politically, as civil war convulsed the city and a vicious oligarchy replaced the democracy in 411. Eventually, after a further seven years of fighting, the Athenians paid a heavy price for their resolute anti-Persianism of the decades from the early 470s on, as Sparta, swallowing its supposed Hellenic love of political liberty, got into bed with the Great King of Persia and received in return the financial wherewithal to construct the victorious fleet that finally brought a starving Athens to its knees in the late winter/early spring of 405–4.

From 404 Sparta, temporarily and so to say unnaturally, assumed the imperial, naval role that Athens had been forced to relinquish, but in the process alienated not only its perennial enemy Athens but even some of its closest mainland Greek allies. So much so that it was forced to fight yet another Greek war, between 395 and 386, in which the Persian gold on offer was this time round being poured into the coffers and pockets of Sparta's collective and individual Greek enemies. At least, that was the case to begin with. By the early 380s, however, the Spartans had seen the error of their ways and begun to seek a renewed rapprochement with the Great King. This they finally and triumphantly achieved in 386—but at a considerable psychological cost. By swearing to a Peace imposed upon them, and in principle upon all other Greeks including the Athenians, by the Great King of Persia, they could justifiably be accused of having medized—taken the part of the Persians. Hence the usual label for this momentous accord: "the King's Peace," whereby the Great King at a stroke reestablished his title to all Asia and undid all the Greeks' territorial and political gains made on that continent since 479. The Spartans themselves rather wittily suggested that the boot was in fact on the other foot—really it was the Medes (Persians) who had "lakonized," that is taken the Spartans' part, since the terms of the peace redounded so blatantly to their differential benefit, at least as regards the other Greeks who were subject to them in mainland European Greece. But that apothegm merely compounded the Spartans' felony, adding insult to injury.

For, as patriotic and deeply disgruntled Athenians saw it, so far was that diplomatic instrument from being suitable to bring about "autonomy" (weasel word implying some kind of freedom and independence) for all Greek cities great and small, as the Spartans proclaimed, that in hard and nasty fact it served as an all too effective instrument for the enslavement of all Greek cities within the direct reach of the Great King of Persia—and for the subordination of those that were not directly reachable to his sycophantic, toadying, un-Greek ally, Sparta. How were the mighty fallen. Compare, or rather contrast, the multiple ways in which their ancestors in their glory days of yore had dealt with the Great King and how in the process they had brought about the genuine autonomy and "freedom" of all Greek cities from the yoke—actual or potential—of the evil Persian empire. Or so Athenian publicists and propagandists of a variety of persuasions and allegiances loudly and insistently proclaimed from at latest 380 BCE (the notional date of the ultraconservative patriot Isocrates' *Panegyric Oration*) onwards.

To prove or at any rate to bolster further this proudly patriotic Athenian, but also Panhellenic, claim or case, a series of supposedly authentic documents was produced—or rather "manufactured"—as evidence. In some cases, the supposed evidence was even digitally enhanced—by human rather than computerized digits, of course. For instance, a "Peace of Callias" (named, like the Peace of Nicias, after the chief negotiator on the Athenian side) was loudly bruited as having been concluded with the Great King, or rather imposed on him by the triumphant Athenians—back in the days of the Athenian maritime supremacy in the Aegean. It is not impossible—and I myself happen to believe—that some informal, pacific agreement was indeed reached between Athens and Persia some time around 450. And the politically and socially well-connected Callias (also super-rich, like Nicias after him, from exploiting mine slaves) could well have fulfilled the role of principal Athenian negotiator. But there is actually no irrefutable evidence for the implementation of any formal treaty until some seventy years after its alleged conclusion. Still less can I accept that the many detailed clauses that suddenly then begin to be bandied about in highly partial and partisan Athenian discourses were all equally authentic. Such, I want to argue, is also the case more or less with the epigraphic Oath of Plataea inscribed on the stele from Acharnae.

The entire monument, including the texts of the two Oaths, was formally a dedication by Dion son of Dion, a priest both of Ares, universal Greek god of war, and of Athena-associated-with-Ares, to those two conjoined deities on behalf of the deme of Acharnae and by extension of the entire city of Athens. (I shall return to these divinities' religious attributes and qualities in the next chapter.) The martial bearing of the monument is conveyed literally from the top down. At the pinnacle of the stele and set in a pediment or gable, so that the whole somewhat conjures up the front elevation of a temple, there are carved in high relief a large round hoplite shield placed dead center and, flanking it, on one side, a helmet and greaves (shin-guards), and, on the other, a cuirass (breastplate) and what may be a military cloak. A sister-inscription to that on our stele records an official fourth-century decree of the deme of Acharnae, relating to the altars of Ares and of Athena Areia (*Supplementum Epigraphicum Graecum* xxi.519). Dion was surely not acting off his own bat. The scene sculpted in relief at the head of this other stele depicts Athena, who is shown wearing her defining military garb of aegis (goatskin breastplate), helmet, and shield, and in the act of crowning a figure of Ares accoutred as a hoplite infantryman. This militarism was both sharply localized at Acharnae and at the same time given a deliberately all-Athenian spin.

Most Greeks, it has been claimed, shuddered when they thought of Ares (see further the next chapter), but for the Athenians of Acharnae at least there seems to have been no such ambivalence about worshipping him, at any rate not outwardly so. Their temple—not located, be it noted, in the city of Athens itself—was not only the sole temple of Ares within the Athenian citizen-state but also one of the very few devoted to Ares anywhere in the extensive Greek world at any time. (Strictly, one should write that it was not located *originally* in the city of Athens, that is, when it was first constructed in the third quarter of the fifth century, roughly contemporaneously with the Parthenon and other major Attic temples. At the end of the first century BCE, however, the temple was actually moved from Acharnae to the center of Athens, piece by piece, and re-erected on newly built foundations just north of the Odeum. This was in the very different political circumstances of the rule over Greece of the Roman emperor Augustus between 27 BCE and 14 CE, for which see chapter 6.) The Acharnians arguably were always keen to exploit this singular local connection, of which the Athenians collectively were very well aware. To explain what I mean by that, let's look briefly at the overall structure of the Athenian democratic state.

Institutionally and legally, since the founding of the democracy in 508/7, acquisition and maintenance of the citizenship of Athens had been made dependent on membership in a deme. That is to say, for a legitimate Athenian adult male to qualify as a citizen he had to be inscribed at the age of majority (eighteen) on the register of one of the 139 or 140 demes (parishes, wards, villages) which together constituted the *polis* or citizen-state of "the Athenians." By a complicated and significantly artificial procedure these 139 or 140 were grouped into thirty *trittues* or "thirdings," which in turn were so combined as to produce ten political "tribes." These demes and tribes were the basis of democratic Athens' political organization—both civilian and military. Each deme had its own assembly, its own property, its own religious cults, and chose officials from among its members, usually by lot and on an annual basis, to administer them all. Each tribe provided 50 councilors, chosen by lot annually, to the central Council of 500, which acted both as the central Assembly's steering committee (at the time of our stele the Assembly met at least 40 times a year, or every nine or so days on average), and also as the permanent executive of the Athenian state. Each tribe, moreover, provided annually one of the board of ten Generals, whose chief executive office covered naval as well as land warfare and had a political as well as purely battlefield function. Generals, exceptionally (like the chief financial officials), were elected rather than chosen by the usual democratic method of appointment to public office, the lot. Each tribe, moreover, furnished one of the ten regiments into which Athens' infantry armies were disposed. Finally, each tribe had a distinct religious identity, celebrating and recording its own cults and festivals.

Acharnae, which was allocated to the tribe Oineis (named after the mythical hero Oeneus), was an unusually large deme; indeed, by size of population rather than in terms of territory it was probably the largest of them all. Thucydides rather remarkably speaks of it as being able to field in 431 no fewer than 3,000 hoplites, which would have constituted about a tenth of the state's entire infantry—including light-armed as well as heavy, noncitizen as well as citizen—all by itself. Aristophanes in an extant comic play originally performed some six years later, early in 425, composed its chorus from and so named the play as a whole precisely after demesmen of Acharnae: *The Acharnians*. In the drama the chorus are represented, presumably with a credible degree of fidelity to fact, as always exceptionally bellicose and unwilling therefore even to contemplate discussing terms of peace with Athens' deadliest enemy, Sparta. Aristophanes' choice of Acharnians, and not any other demesmen, was no doubt due at least in part to the unique existence of the shrine and temple of Ares (with Athena Areia) at Acharnae.

The concatenation of Ephebes and Plataea on our document is further grist to this overtly military mill. The universal Greek term *ephêbos* meant literally "on the threshold of full adult age," and different Greek cities construed it differently in terms of actual physical age. In Athens it meant those eighteen and nineteen years old, although eighteen was also the age of full civic and political maturity in terms of eligibility to attend the Assembly and vote under the Athenian democracy. There are hints that perhaps already in the fifth century, and at any rate by the 370s, the Athenians had taken the trouble to organize some sort of military training for the two year–classes of citizens who had attained the age of bare civic majority, eighteen, but were not yet deemed to be fully adult, at twenty. It is pretty certain that there was associated with such training an original and possibly quite early Ephebic Oath, not unlike the version recorded on our stele, although I would myself allow for modifications being introduced over time. However, a step-change in the military training of eighteen- and nineteen-year-old proto-citizens was signaled in the mid-330s by the formal introduction, through a law attributed to one Epicrates, of what is known for short as the Ephebeia. That is to say, a centrally planned and regulated system of "national service" was introduced at Athens, hardly coincidentally, soon after the Athenians' disastrous defeat at Chaeronea in Boeotia at the hands of Philip and Alexander's Macedonians in 338. Lycurgus was not the official instigator of this new training regime, but, given its deeply patriotic implications and resonances, his guiding hand behind it, as behind much of official Athenian policy during the whole decade from 336 to 326, may easily be suspected, indeed detected.

Above all, there is the example to him of the Spartans, who had anticipated the Athenians by centuries in this matter of public military education and training. Indeed, they had long ago introduced a centrally directed and compulsory educational cycle for males from the age of seven upwards, which segued organically between the ages of twelve and fourteen into the sort of "ephebic" training that the Athenians were only now beginning to implement for those eighteen and nineteen years old. Now, Sparta in that respect was unique in all Greece, and of course by the 330s the state was but a shadow of its former military self. Traditionally too, admiration for Spartan ways had come only from Athenians who were less than one-hundred-percent democratic in their political outlook. However, there are reasons for thinking that Sparta—a much earlier, gloriously efficient, Plataea-winning Sparta—was indeed the indirect inspiration for this Athenian, later fourth-century innovation, and that the presiding genius of the move was Lycurgus. In his one surviving major political speech he explicitly mentioned an alleged—but transparently mythical—connection between early Athens and Sparta's precocious prowess as a military state. Lycurgus was himself an aristocrat, from a long-established priestly family, and bore moreover a famously Spartan name. (Sparta's Lycurgus was credited with having played the role of his city's Founding Father, many centuries ago.) It seems to me therefore plausible to suggest that there was a central and unifying thought behind reproducing the oath sworn by the Ephebes (both before the mid-330s and with renewed institutional salience from the mid-330s) and the Oath of Plataea together one after the other on the same stele within a religious document addressed in part to the city-protecting goddess in her martial aspect. This thought was the literally pious hope that Athens' ephebes would be inspired to reproduce the putative glory of their ancestors at Plataea, borrowed—or stolen— though that glory was, at least in part, from its true owners, the Spartans.

CONCLUSION: POSSIBLE SCENARIOS

The shrine and temple at Acharnae were devoted mainly if not solely to Ares, but by associating with him the militarized version of the patron goddess of the entire city of Athens the priest Dion (whose own name is derived from that of Athena's father, Zeus) was presumably hoping to endow his offering with a wider, all-Athenian significance and implication. I have even wondered whether Dion might not have been ordered to associate, perhaps by Lycurgus himself or by his presumed associate Epicrates, a peculiarly martial Athena with Ares. Alternatively, Dion or his like-minded supporters may themselves have taken the initiative and, precisely through erecting this remarkable monument, dropped a huge hint as to the need for some major military-educational reform. For I am inclined to think there is some direct connection between the erection of this expensive and striking monument, which I would like to place in the two to three years immediately after the battle of Chaeronea in 338, and the introduction of the formal ephebate in c. 335. That would by itself explain the transcription here of a current version of the Ephebic oath. Adding to it a version of the supposedly ancient but in fact much more recently cobbled together Oath of Plataea, its instigators might well have thought, would serve both to link present and future with glorious past—and help viewers and auditors somehow to get over the awfulness of the all too recent and still vividly and painfully memorable debacle at Chaeronea.

3

———

THE PLATAEA OATH AS A DOCUMENT OF ANCIENT GREEK RELIGION

The same oath is not equal for the impious and the pious

—Xenophanes of Colophon, sixth–fifth century BCE

To read the Oath of Plataea as an item of quasi-nationalistic propaganda is only one of the many possible interpretations of the meanings of this multivalent Oath when it is studied as a document of its own time. The other main interpretative avenue that I shall now explore in particular is the religious.

The ancient pagan (pre-Christian) world was full of religious oaths. So much so that the practice provoked the sharpest possible retort and rebuke from Christianity's titular

Founder himself (*Matthew* ch. V verses 33–37, King James 1611 Version):

> Again, ye have heard that it hath been said by them
> of old time, Thou
> shalt not forswear thyself, but shalt perform unto
> the Lord thine oaths: But
> I say unto you, Swear not at all: neither by heaven:
> for it is God's throne:
> Nor by the earth: for it is his footstool: neither by
> Jerusalem: for it is the
> city of the great King. Neither shalt thou swear by
> thy head, because
> thou canst not make one hair white or black. But let
> your communication
> be, Yea, yea; Nay, nay: for whatsoever is more than
> these cometh of evil.

That's telling them! But the ancient Athenians and other Greeks of the third quarter of the fourth century BCE, living some 400 years earlier than this Gospel text and in an entirely different mental and spiritual universe, could not have begun to understand what Christos ("the anointed one," a Greek translation of the Hebrew term) was getting so steamed up about. For them, swearing oaths—with the inevitable corollary of forswearing and being forsworn from time to time—was almost as natural or second-nature as breathing. And the scope for doing so, in terms of the availability of divine bodies by whom to swear an oath, was almost limitless.

Hence, on the cornice of the pediment of our stele is inscribed the one word "Gods"—which for ancient Greeks included goddesses. The Greeks were radical polytheists, even though that wasn't a word they themselves used, let alone coined. That literally theo-logical invocation sets the overall religious tone of the text, comprising two oaths, that follows. In fact, as noted, oaths were a very prevalent part of ancient Greek culture and society, and this had been the case from the poems of Homer (c. 700 BCE) on. Their deep and central significance may be accurately measured by the fact that the chief Olympian deity who was thought to preside over their swearing and observance (and punish their nonobservance) was none other than the chief Olympian deity himself, great father Zeus, here worshipped under the grand title of Horkios ("Oath-Controller"). So, when a Greek read "Gods" on the Acharnae stele, he or she may well have had Zeus primarily in mind, although the god of the shrine to whom his priest made this dedication was actually Ares in association with Zeus's daughter Athena, conceived in her martial guise (of whom more anon).

To try to pin down the nature of the Plataea Oath more precisely, we shall consider first a couple of cross-cultural comparisons that may help to bring out some of the specificities of ancient Greek oath-swearing, and then a number of variously relevant ancient Greek *comparanda*, using a small selection of representative Athenian examples. In 2010, American documentary filmmaker and producer Laura Poitras made "The Oath," an exploration of the inner lives of some Al-Qaeda jihadists. Oaths, that is to say, can still be highly meaningful today, but they are particularly so among certain sworn brotherhoods that set themselves apart from and, indeed, are in violent opposition to mainstream society. Conversely, to track back to the European Middle Ages, there we find that oath-swearing was rather a common, mainstream method of seeking to obtain or to ensure legal justice. That was preeminently true in the case of mediaeval England's compact between King John and his barons sworn at Runnymede near Windsor in 1215, a compact known commonly as the "Magna Carta" (and still not without political-legal relevance today). I quote from Article 60 (in a translation that aims to capture the sense rather than the precise wording of the original Latin):

> Any man who so desires may take an oath to obey the commands of the twenty-five [newly elected] barons for the achievement of these ends, and to join with them in assailing us [King John] to the utmost of his power. We give public and free permission to take this oath to any man who so desires.... Indeed, we will compel any of our subjects who are unwilling to take it to swear it at our command.

None of the "signatories" (swearers) to the supposed Oath of Plataea was under any such royal compulsion. *Au contraire*: the swearer states had all, *ex hypothesi*, united willingly and voluntarily to resist a foreign "barbarian" monarch, the sort who did not scruple to send his envoys into Hellenic territory with a regal and indeed imperious Persian-style demand for "earth and water." Yet the Plataea Oath was no less sworn in the sight of and under the authority of an overridingly awesome divine power than was Magna Carta. For the Greeks, divine authority was not necessarily seen as incompatible with free political and military association between equals. Yet, as in the European Middle Ages, so in ancient Greece unidirectional and hierarchical divine and secular authority might sometimes also be considered mutually reinforcing, as we shall see.

For, turning now to some ancient Greek examples, we find that in the 440s BCE the imperial Athenians imposed a treaty of settlement on the island city of Eretria, after putting down a serious attempt by the Eretrians (and other Euboean islanders) to revolt from what they considered an unacceptably unequal military alliance—dominated by Athens and directed formally against Persia. On the stone as it survives to this day the text ends:

(Resolved that) an oath be taken by the (Athenian) Generals, the Council and the Cavalrymen [or "Knights"] of the Athenians and by the generals, the Council, and the other officials of the Eretrians.

This treaty-oath obliged both parties to uphold the terms of the settlement under pain of retributive punishment from the gods if either broke them. The swearing of such an oath was the ancient Greeks' functional equivalent of our "signing" a treaty, except that the oath was strictly religious and conferred a binding sanctity of divine authorization that our formula typically lacks.

To turn from interstate power relations to civic relations within a single citizen-state, let us consider the Athenians' popular jury courts, which were an essential arena of their democratic governance and decision-making. The 6,000 citizens who were impanelled as potential jurors randomly by lot every year were literally sworn in: that is, they took an oath to give their verdicts impartially in accordance with the laws and decrees of the Athenian People. In an age lacking both forensic science and any otherwise unimpeachable, objectively reliable evidence, both the principals and the witnesses in a court case swore that the evidence they gave was nothing but the truth, and this oath was considered to be the fundamental probative argument since no one willingly and knowingly would wish to perjure himself, given the certainty of divine punishment that would surely follow the transgressor. As the second-century CE traveler-pilgrim Pausanias of Magnesia put it (4.22.7): "it is hard for a perjured man to escape the notice of a god"—the god in question here being Zeus Lycaeus ("of Mount Lycaeum" in Arcadia). That pious observation would have risen unbidden to the lips of any fifth- or fourth-century BCE Athenian too, though it was prompted in Pausanias by the fate of one Aristocrates, whom the Arcadians stoned to death and whose corpse they cast beyond the frontiers without burial, damning his memory into the bargain. Visibility of exemplary punishment was deemed key here to the efficacy of the ritualized perjury-punishment complex.

But perhaps in some ways even more relevant and apposite for appreciating the Oath of Plataea was the oath that all athletes and judges swore at the commencement of each new Olympic Games in the regular, four-year cycle. The patron of those Games was also Zeus, here the Zeus of Mount Olympus, the same mighty father Zeus who carried the title Horkios. He presided at Olympia over games that were by definition Panhellenic: that is, all and only Greeks might compete in them, and the judges of the contests—always drawn solely from the nearby city of Elis—were entitled Hellanodikai or "Judges of the Greeks." The Battle of Plataea and its Oath, whatever the historicity of the latter might have been, were also quintessentially "Panhellenic" matters.

Finally, so far as oaths and oath-taking are concerned, one interesting religious aspect of the Plataea battle and its aftermath that deserves mention here is the one that has been discussed very well by Deborah Boedeker (2007). She noticed that in Herodotus all canonical victories over Persians, including the Battle of Plataea, have an Eleusinian connection. In Boeotia, the sanctuary of Demeter near Plataea (9.57.2, 62.2) had indeed a specifically Spartan connection, but the famous Panhellenic sanctuary of Demeter and her daughter (Kore/Persephone), the site of the Eleusinian Mysteries, was located at Eleusis in Attica. If the hunch is correct that some sort of authentic ancestor of the Acharnae Oath was indeed sworn before the battle of Plataea, then the site of Eleusis, where the Spartan-led forces under Pausanias joined up with the Athenians under Aristeides, would indeed have carried the requisitely sanctified and Panhellenic aura.

Let us look next at the various gods and other divine powers invoked by name in the Acharnae stele oaths. Ares was the religious personification of war, as auditors or readers of Homer needed no reminding. Yet, given that he was both a fully-fledged and regular member of the pantheon of both male and female immortals who were supposed to dwell eternally together on the peak of Mt. Olympus (the highest mountain in Greece), and given moreover that he was the war-god of a culture seemingly devoted to endemic warfare, it is rather surprising to say the least to find that ancient Greeks' appreciation of Ares was marked by an abiding ambivalence.

In Homer's *Iliad*, one of the ancient Greeks' foundational cultural artifacts, Ares is dubbed "most hateful . . . of all the gods who hold Olympus" (book 5, line 890). This hatred might be explained by his unfortunate tendency to sanction the deaths of one's friends and loved ones as much as those of one's deadly enemies, but all the same one would have expected to find him a little loved, however toughly, as well as hated. Even for the notably martial, indeed bellicose national poet of the Spartans, Tyrtaeus (mid-seventh century), he was "lamentable Ares" (Tyrt. 11.7, cf. 12.34, 19.4), which echoes a sentiment expressed not much earlier by the other Greek national poet beside Homer, Hesiod from Ascra in Boeotia (c. 700 BCE). He too ascribed to Ares "lamentable works" and "deeds of violence" (*hubris*: *Works and Days* line 145), very much the sorts of things to be associated with an Iron Age of the seemingly interminable present that in Hesiod's notably pessimistic worldview had irrevocably replaced an irretrievably lost Golden Age.

The goddess Athena (in Greek, Athene) came with no such negative baggage. Of course, there was not just one homogeneous, all-purpose Athena, but rather many different Athenas, many of them worshipped officially within and by the state of Athens. The most important of them all, politically speaking, was the Athena surnamed Polias, literally "of the

City," meaning city-holding or city-protecting Athena. Every four years, the deliberately primitive-looking olivewood statue that was understood to incarnate her was draped ceremonially with a fancily woven new robe. This ceremony was one of the most essential components of a huge religious pageant known as the Great or City Panathenaea that variously involved all the different classes of inhabitants of both the city itself (including the port city of Peiraieus) and the surrounding countryside. Closely allied to Athena Polias were two other Athenas, both also prominently represented on her most holy of holy spots within Attica, the Athenian Acropolis or High City. One was Athena the "front-rank fighter" (Promachus), the other Athena the Virgin (Parthenos). In both guises she was represented as if she were an adult male hoplite warrior, bearing spear, shield, and her own peculiar version of a breastplate (a magic goatskin or *aigis*, whence our "aegis"). This is a salutary reminder that Athena, though female, was not exactly feminine, and indeed that Greek gods and goddesses are more accurately viewed as collections of superhuman powers rather than genuinely human in spirit, for all their representation and worship in anthropomorphic—human-shape—form.

For Athena Promachus, Phidias, the greatest sculptor of his—and many others'—day, had created a stupendous bronze statue located at the very entrance to the Acropolis. For Athena Parthenos, the Athenians under the guidance of Pericles had erected a huge and magnificent temple, the Parthenon, around whose central rooms ran a 160-meter frieze filled with splendid relief sculpture. It is generally believed today that the religious procession that is the main subject of the frieze somehow alludes to—rather than directly depicts—the procession of the Great or City Panathenaea mentioned just above. Again, Phidias was given a major role to play, fashioning the massive chryselephantine (gold and ivory on a wooden core) cult-statue of the Virgin—different in every possible way from the basic statue of the Polias. For the same Panathenaic festival huge numbers of a special type of olive oil storage jar ("Panathenaic amphora") were created every four years to serve as prizes in the athletic and other contests; and on these jars, the goddess herself was depicted on one side, resplendent in full martial rig, associated with the particular event depicted on the other face. Hence, the association of Athena with Ares in the form invoked by the Acharnians—Athena as Ares—was entirely acceptable, even predictable, on military grounds.

Not so predictable, perhaps, are the various divinities or quasi-divinities invoked as witnesses—and so enforcers—of the supposedly ancestral oath of the ephebes:

> Aglaurus, Hestia, Enyo, Enyalius, Ares and Athena Areia, Zeus, Thallo, Auxo, Hegemone, Heracles, boundaries of the fatherland, wheat crops, barley crops, vines, olives, figs.

Appeal to crops and to boundaries, as if they were gods and goddesses, has been found odd, especially when it goes in conjunction with appeal to more normal, anthropomorphic Olympian deities. But against that view I would argue, in part at least, by pointing to the devastation caused by the foreign invasion and occupation of Attica during the horribly prolonged Atheno-Peloponnesian War of the later fifth century (431–404, especially 413–404). Since then, as a direct response, the Athenians had put a lot more effort into constructing what one modern historian has called "Fortress Attica" (Ober 1985), concentrating at first on land boundaries both at the limits of and within Attica, the territory of the Athenian city-state. Moreover, frontiers were often deemed to be sacred in Greece, even if it was only the minutely pious Spartans who are known to have devised specific "frontier-crossing" religious rituals (*diabatêria*). Thus frontiers had to be sanctified as well as patrolled in a secular way. Moreover, it is not impossible that one particularly impressive frontier vallation—the Dema Wall extending between Mount Aigaleos and Mount Parnes in the pass between the plain of Eleusis and the plain of Athens—was constructed precisely in the immediate aftermath of Chaeronea—notionally the very moment that provoked also our emblematic monument.

Of the remaining elements, however, one, the first to be listed, was not just appropriate but indeed inevitable. In myth Aglaurus was the daughter of one of Athens' very first kings, Cecrops, who had thrown herself from the (very high) Acropolis as a symbolic sacrifice in order to save the city from a hostile invasion. The real-life Athenian ephebes were called upon, likewise, to save the city, and it was in the holy sanctuary of Aglaurus on the slope below the east end of the Acropolis that the ephebes—as an admittedly much later source reports—swore their collective and communal oath.

In short, the Oath of Plataea, like the collocated ephebic oath, is a religious oath, sworn by the Athenians in the name of the gods, who would be sure to punish the transgressors if in any way the Oath's prescriptions should be violated or ignored. More specifically still, the Athenians had hereby supposedly laid upon themselves a religious curse (*ara*), the point of that being to make clear that any transgression of the oath by them would automatically incur religious pollution (*agos*). *Agos* could have a wide range of occasions and manifestations. For example, if a Spartan master exacted from his Helots (serf-like "slave" workers) more of his land's produce by way of rent than he had contractually agreed to, he would automatically fall subject to an *agos* that would need somehow to be expiated by an act of cleansing. It may well be felt by us that such illegal treatment of a Helot was as nothing compared to actually murdering him or her—yet the Spartans themselves also allowed for, indeed encouraged that eventuality, in a typically pious way. At the start of each new civil year their chief civil officials, the Ephors ("Overseers"), ritually declared all Helots to be "enemies," precisely so that they might legitimately be murdered without their killer's having to fear incurring the automatic religious pollution that would otherwise have accrued to any act of killing another human being outside battle. On the other hand, if one Greek citizen killed another fellow citizen, for example in a civil war, then the ritual consequences could be dire—as was the case for the Aiginetans, as described in a chapter of Herodotus's sixth book (6.91).

This is one of several instances in Herodotus of what the Greeks called *stasis* or internal division, meaning literally a process of—deadly hostile—"standing" apart from and over against each other, in civil strife or civil war. Herodotus

personally had suffered from this in his home city of Halicarnassus, and in his own voice he issued a loud and memorable
protest against it:

> Division within a kindred people (*stasis emphulios*) is
> as much worse than a united war against an external
> enemy as war is worse than peace. (8.3.1)

In about 491 the Aiginetans' civil strife had taken the form of
a struggle between the ordinary poor citizens and the elite few
rich citizens who controlled and ran the wealthy island city.
The rich captured 700 of the poor and were preparing a mass
execution of them when one of the prisoners broke free and
sought sanctuary—asylum—in a temple of Demeter the Lawgiver (Thesmophoros). He managed to grab the latch of the
temple door but couldn't open it and get to safety inside in
time before the elite were upon him. Failing to pry his fingers
away, they simply cut off his hands and carried him off with
what were formerly his hands still sticking to the latch. Demeter, however, was not amused or pleased. Pollution (*agos*) was
visited not just upon the immediate perpetrators but upon all
Aiginetans for a very long time to come, since "they were not
able to expiate the curse by performing sacrifice, even though
they tried all sorts of ways of eliminating it." Indeed, they were
still under a curse sixty years later, when their Athenian enemies evicted them from the island and resettled them in the
eastern Peloponnese. Pollution in ancient Greece could take
many forms—there was even more than one term for the con-
dition, the most common being *miasma*. In a state of religious

uncleanliness Greeks were unable to conduct normal everyday relations with the gods on whose beneficence everything—fertility, the weather, happiness—ultimately depended. In this case, as Herodotus clearly seems to imply without actually stating, it was precisely because they were still polluted by that curse that Demeter allowed them to be evicted from their island by the Athenians—and so to be deprived permanently of their homes and homeland, entailing separation from the gods and the graves of their ancestors. This form of civic death was considered to be among the severest of all punishments in Greek eyes.

CONCLUSION: HOW TO AVOID *STASIS*, ATHENIAN-STYLE

It must be stressed first therefore that the piety of the Plataea oath-swearers in this regard is generically Hellenic, not peculiarly Athenian. Yet, following on directly from that Aigina story of Herodotus, I would want at once to add that it is a kind of piety to which Athenians perhaps were of necessity especially inclined. For few Greeks knew better than they the risks and costs of *stasis*. A brief history of *stasis* at Athens through the centuries will at least illustrate and perhaps also corroborate that suggestion.

As early as the 630s (the time of a failed attempt at seizing a dictatorship made by Olympic victor Cylon) *stasis* had afflicted Athens severely, as it did so again at the turn of the sixth century, when moderate citizen Solon was selected precisely as *diallaktês* ("arbitrator"), tasked with a mission to reconcile competing interest groups. The divisive issues of the day were religious and economic in nature as well as political in a more narrowly defined sense. Solon's solution did indeed work for a while, but in the 550s and more especially in the last two decades of the sixth century *stasis* broke out at Athens fiercely once again. The resolution of 508/7 marked the introduction of democracy or proto-democracy at least, but not quite the abolition of *stasis* or all tendencies toward it. The institution of the odd device of ostracism—attributed to democracy's founder Cleisthenes—was one way of letting steam out of the pressure cooker of Athenian democratic politics. Every year Athenians were asked whether they wished to hold an ostracism (a kind of reverse election); if they did so wish, on the appointed day they brought potsherds (*ostraka*) bearing the name of their preferred "candidate" to the central Agora, where they were counted, and, so long as there was a quorum of 6,000 valid votes cast, the candidate who received the most negative votes was declared an exile—without loss of citizen status or property—for the next ten years. An extreme form of political death for an ambitious politician.

But an even better expedient altogether for knocking competing Athenian heads together was mutual and collective fear of an external enemy—such as the Persians proved to be. To meet the invasion of 480, ostracized politicians were recalled and even reinstated in offices, and all Athenians found themselves literally as well as metaphorically in the same boats as they evacuated their city completely not once but twice, in 479 as well as 480, and horrifyingly witnessed it—and especially its holy places and objects—being smashed by barbarian hands. Small wonder that "holy Salamis" was so fervently recalled and revered in the stunningly victorious aftermath (chapter 6). Yet within a generation a leading democratic reformer, Ephialtes, was assassinated (462/1 BCE), and some four to five years later there was rumor of an oligarchic fifth column within Athens willing to surrender the (democratic) city to the discretion of a jealously competitive and very anti-democratic Sparta.

That threat was at least postponed for many decades, but only under the cover and at the cost of a major war, the Greeks' equivalent of a world war, and one that also greatly exacerbated internal Athenian political and social tensions: the Atheno-Peloponnesian War of 431 to 404 BCE. In his brilliant *History of the Peloponnesian War* Thucydides the Athenian devoted great pains to a clinical analysis of *stasis*, its origins, motivations and modalities, taking as his main case study an outbreak on the island of Corcyra in 427 but dealing also with the oligarchically driven *stasis* that crippled Athens in 411. The rationalist author typically gave very little space indeed in all his preserved work to religion as such, but one notable exception concerns his depiction of the Spartan Brasidas. On him Thucydides not only conferred a great deal of attention but even showered praise for his being a "not bad (i.e., exceptionally able) public speaker, for a Spartan." In Thucydides' version of a speech Brasidas delivered to the Acanthians of northern Greece in 422 he credibly has Brasidas making great play with the Spartans' (allegedly) regular practice of abiding by their oaths.

In sharp contrast, as Thucydides' continuator Xenophon (c. 427–354) and the much later biographer Plutarch (c. 46–120 CE) make plain, Lysander, the Spartan commander who did most to win the Peloponnesian War for Sparta, notoriously made light of the sanctity—and presumably the efficacy—of oaths. One cheats boys with knucklebones, he is reputed to have said, but men with oaths. Now, Lysander not only played the equivalent of Regent Pausanias in the Graeco-Persian Wars. He was also a most vigorous stirrer of faction, which he fomented in the interests of installing as rulers in key cities of Sparta's new post-Athenian empire his own fierce ideological partisans, all men of a diehard oligarchic persuasion. Such was the case, inevitably, of defeated Athens itself. Here, a collective tyranny of thirty oligarchic ultras, backed by a Spartan garrison on the Acropolis, terrorized Athens for a year, until the Thirty fell out among themselves and Athenian democratic exiles managed to raise a sufficient force of liberation from outside to join with the democrats at home to fight and win a very nasty civil war.

One, absolutely key way in which the Athenians dragged themselves out of the mire of civil bloodshed and internecine hatred was by imposing upon themselves a great oath, an oath of forgetting—or, as they put it the other way round, "not-remembering." That is, in the sight of the gods as witnesses, they publicly and collectively threw a veil over the black deeds of especially those Athenians who in a frenzy of ideological madness had embraced the most extreme form of anti-democracy. Strict observance of this oath of Amnesty was put under great strain in the coming decades, but nonetheless it did still, just, hold. Even non- or anti-democrats such as Xenophon were loud in their praise of the Athenians for that achievement, and rightly so. Moreover, the democratic Athenians, unlike many other Greeks of the fourth century BC, such as those in democratic Argos for a conspicuous instance, did not again fall into *stasis*—until, that is, both their autonomy and their democracy were successively removed by the Macedonian overlords of all mainland Greece in the 330s and 320s BCE.

Athenians, therefore, could be said to have had a special affinity, and affection, for oaths, particularly oaths that fostered amity and collective endeavor, and particularly in the *stasis*-ridden atmosphere of the fourth century BCE. An oath such as the supposed Oath of Plataea fitted very neatly into this ideological-political domestic context, where it reinforced the tendency of the Athenians to cast themselves as the sole true champions of free and independent Hellenism in the face, on the one hand, of the Spartan and Theban traitors, and, on the other, the monstrous Persian imperial juggernaut.

4

THE PERSIAN WARS

Making History on Oath with Herodotus

. . . so that human events do not fade with time
—Herodotus (*Histories*, Preface, trans. A. Purvis 2007)

TELLING THE PAST'S HISTORY

All history, arguably, is contemporary history. That is to say, to some extent, and in some way or ways, it is the historian who makes out of the surviving, accessible record of past events and processes a history that is meaningful in and for the present. Put differently, the past—what actually happened, and what can be retrieved of all that did happen—is one thing. A history of a past—what is considered to be significant enough to be written up into a historical work, and the way it should be done—is quite another. Each and every historian's history will—must—differ somehow, significantly, from every other.

In a powerful sense therefore all history is also subjective, but any historian worth her or his salt will always choose a subject that is sufficiently well documented and sufficiently important, and write it up in a sufficiently attractive, indeed engaging, way, for an audience of considerably more than one. The first western historian properly and fully to earn the title of "historian" is Herodotus of Halicarnassus (now Bodrum, on the Aegean coast of western Turkey), and it is partly for that reason that I chose an extract from his pathbreaking "Preface" for the epigraph of this chapter (see Fig. 4.1). But only partly: because it so happens that the subject of the present book is also a key aspect of Herodotus's own chosen life work, which was designed both to investigate and to celebrate and commemorate the history of relations between Greeks and non-Greek "barbarians," especially the Persians and their empire. Above all else, what Herodotus enquired about with a view to exposing and expounding was the history—or rather a history, his version—of why they came to fight against one another during the two decades between 499 and 479. And he did so because he believed implicitly that that East-West conflict was a permanently decisive clash of civilizations, not just an encounter of local, purely Greek significance.

An awful lot of our understanding of the Persian Wars—not just of the facts, supposed, but also of their interpretation—has to depend on how we read Herodotus. If—as is the case here—he does not mention an occurrence that is mentioned

Figure 4.1. A non-veristic idealized image of the "Father of History,"
Herodotus, whose Histories ("Researches") is the ultimate basis of any
subsequent account of the Graeco-Persian Wars. Gianni Dagli Orti/The
Art Archive at Art Resource, NY.

in other sources, or—as is also the case here—he mentions
a comparable occurrence but at a different juncture from that
presented in other sources, what weight are we to give to the

discrepancies? To be specific, and cut to the chase, Herodotus does not mention an oath sworn by the Greeks before Plataea, but he does mention one sworn before Thermopylae. What should we make of that? On balance, I have decided that, had a major oath been sworn before Plataea, he should and would have mentioned it then and there (see further chapter 6). But I confess I have less confidence in that view than I do in the claim that, but for Herodotus, we could not begin to write anything worthy of the name of "history" about the Graeco-Persian Wars as a whole, and as such. It is against that conceptual and interpretative backdrop that the following brief and tentative summary account should be read.

The military aspects of those relations between Greeks and non-Greeks that Herodotus set himself to enquire into, above all the battles of 490 (Marathon), 480 (Thermopylae, Artemisium, and Salamis), and 479 BCE (Plataea and Mycale), are conventionally referred to collectively as "The Persian Wars." But that is because, traditionally, they have been seen more or less exclusively from the (or a) Greek point of view, as the Wars against the Persians. Far better in my view to label them the "Graeco-Persian Wars" since that is a label that at least starts to bring out their complexly interrelated dynamic duality. Actually, the situation was more complicated even than that. It was not a simple case of Greeks on one side fighting against non-Greeks, and most particularly Persians, on the other. Actually, more Greeks fought on the Persian side than fought against the Persians: partly under compulsion as subjects of Persia, partly out of a prudent, self-interested, non-ideological calculation that Persia would likely emerge as victor. It is one of

Herodotus' very greatest merits as an interested but largely objective reporter and analyst that, so far from writing "official" history or mere propaganda, he does nothing to disguise the internal conflicts that constantly threatened to undermine the far from wholehearted as well as perilously thinly spread Greek resistance.

If history is proverbially written by the victors, in this present case that is all too literally true. The Achaemenid Persians seem never to have written history in anything like a Herodotean sense. Although their many subjects included Jews, and a few books of the Hebrew and later Bibles (*Esther*, *Nehemiah*, *Ezra*) do refer to events and processes directly related to the management of the Persian empire, these too do not constitute history, even in the loose sense of the word that might be applied to the theologically loaded biblical narrative books of *Kings* and *Chronicles*. What the Persians did produce in written and fortunately enduring form, and in considerable quantities, were bureaucratic documents incised on clay in several languages, including Greek—so that we thereby know a good deal about the workings of Persian imperial administration and, yet more important, we gain access to the very *arcanum* of the Achaemenid Persian empire, namely that at its heart it was a bureaucrat's dream. Besides such written testimony, the Achaemenids left behind—to be retrieved by archaeologists from the nineteenth century up to the present day—a formidable repertoire of artworks in multiple media, not least finely crafted vessels in gold and silver and a distinctively powerful imperial style of architecture that drew creatively upon the traditions of several ancient and conquered peoples, foremost the

Egyptians and Assyrians. However, for all their many other merits, archaeology's tools are intrinsically dumb. The pick and spade, etc. may not be able to tell a lie, but that's partly because they cannot speak and have to be spoken for when it comes to interpreting the material culture they deal in specifically; and that can be done in various, often contradictory ways. The remains that they uncover are, moreover, not always in themselves unambiguous enough to tell us what they are remains of, let alone what social, political, economic, religious, and other functions they had served. To take an admittedly extreme instance, the Tall-e Takht, an unfinished stone platform at Pasargadae in southern Iran, the Persian empire's original capital, has been interpreted variously as a prison and as the mausoleum of the Persian founder Cyrus the Great's mother.

Of the battles cited above, Plataea was the decisive one, a victory for the relative handful of "loyalist" Greek cities united, under Sparta's overall leadership and command in the field, to resist a massive attempt by Persia to incorporate mainland Greece into its vast empire. In order to understand the nature and place of that battle in ancient and world history, we must first set the scene by describing the rise and development of the two principal antagonists: on the one side, the Achaemenid Persian empire (holding intercontinental sway over territory stretching from the Indus river valley to southeastern Europe, and from the Aral Sea region to northeast Africa); on the other, "the Greeks"—a convenient misnomer for a motley and small selection from the hundreds of Greek cities that made up what they called "Hellas," the Greek-speaking and Greek-thinking world.

THE ACHAEMENID PERSIAN EMPIRE

The empire takes its modern name from a supposed eponym of the ruling house, Achaemenes, but we have no independent corroboration of the existence claimed for him by Emperor Darius I, who from 522/1 to 486 BCE ruled in his name and in that of the great Iranian god of Light and Truth, Ahura-Mazda. "By the favor of Ahura-Mazda I hold this kingship," proclaims Darius on an extremely long and extremely inaccessible trilingual proclamation chiseled on a commanding rock face at Bisitun in northern Iran, giving his own version of how he came to be king in the first place. Darius was in fact only the empire's second founder. It had been originally established by the extraordinary Cyrus II "the Great" in about 550 BCE and within a generation or two had leapt beyond its Iranian base to embrace central Asia, the rest of Asia as far east as Pakistan, Egypt in north Africa, and in Europe a chunk of northern Greece and the north shore of the Aegean up to the Hellespont (Dardanelles) besides.

Herodotus preserves a fascinating and pioneering exercise in political theory, which he rather implausibly believed to be historically authentic, in which three leading Persians in c. 520 solemnly debated the pros and cons of Rule by One *versus* Rule by Some and Rule by All. Actually, an empire such as the Achaemenid Persian could only ever have been ruled by an absolute autocratic monarch, and the supposed debate makes much more sense as an early, perhaps the very earliest known, example of Greek political theorizing about rival modes of political rule. At any rate, the triumph of the monarchical argument in the supposed debate is echoed, unsurprisingly, by the triumph in actual political practice of all-powerful monarchs such as first Cyrus and then, following a massive crisis of confidence at the heart of the imperial government in the late 520s, Darius proved themselves to be. Not backward in coming forward, Cyrus (reigned 558–530) had himself referred to in the famous "Cyrus Cylinder" (written in Akkadian cuneiform; it comes from Babylon but is now in the British Museum's collection) as follows: "King of the world, great king, legitimate king, king of Babylon, king of Sumer and Akkad, king of the four rims of the earth . . . of a family which always exercised kingship, whose rule [the gods] love. . . ." And not only the gods: the Jews who found themselves restored to their native land after three to four generations of captivity "by the waters of Babylon" hailed him, as a Messiah no less. Cyrus's son Cambyses (reigned 525–522), Darius (reigned c. 522–486) and his son Xerxes (reigned 486–65), and the other notionally Achaemenid successors were scarcely more modest than Cyrus, but perhaps they could not have been expected quite to live up to the Founder's exemplary achievements.

It is not quite clear what the official religion of the Persian empire was—apart from the predominance of Ahura-Mazda and the existence of at least a prototype of Zoroastrianism, according to which the world consisted of and was contested between eternally opposed powers of Light and Darkness, of Truth and the Lie. What is clear is that no official religion was imposed upon all Persia's subjects indiscriminately; rather, respect was normally shown on the part of the center for divergent local custom and belief. Moreover, despite the Greeks' possibly willful misunderstanding of the Persian court protocol of obeisance, the King was not himself considered to be a divine being but instead was regarded and approached as a kind of supreme human manifestation and agent on earth of the divine sphere. A combination of surviving words and images makes abundantly plain that the overarching, driving ideology of the Persian monarchy and empire was one of what John Lewis has aptly called "magnificent dominance," a divinely sanctioned ideology of "expanding royal supremacy." Believing in that set Persia on a collision course with the Greek cities that lay at and immediately beyond the western margins of its imperial bailiwick. Xerxes, the Great King who occupied the throne of the Achaemenid dynasty in 479, had, like his father Darius I before him, and his father-in-law Cyrus before him, "to demonstrate his power and to expand it—the ideology, and the success of his rule, demanded it" (Lewis 2010: 24; cf. 15, 17).

Yet not even the most charismatic and authoritative autocrat can rule alone, and the Great King's rule was elaborately buttressed and potently expressed through a finely tuned and sharply honed bureaucracy focused on the great palatial centers of Pasargadae, the chief administrative capital Susa, and (as the Greeks called it) Persepolis (the two latter due initially to Darius I)—all of these sites situated in southern Iran—and Ecbatana, modern Hamadan, located in Media farther north in Iran. Lucky finds of caches of bureaucratic documents written on baked clay in Elamite (a local Iranian language), Old Persian, and other languages including Greek reveal the inner workings of the bureaucracy. In particular, they minutely document the hierarchical gradations of persons and status that were nicely calibrated by measuring the amounts of rations to be doled out from the central storehouses. These rations were in some cases the substance of mere life or livelihood, but in others they were the underpinnings of lifestyles, some of them inordinately grandiose, especially when judged by the Greeks' much humbler standards. (A proverbial Greek saying had it that Greece and Poverty were foster-sisters; Persians for their part allegedly could not understand how the Greeks could get by with eating so little.) The empire's official language was not Elamite or any other Iranian language but Aramaic, a member of the Semitic language family and later the language of Yeshua (also known as Jesus) of Galilee. One baked clay document written in Aramaic around 500 BCE well illustrates the empire's geographical reach, as it tracks travelers using the amazing Persian long-distance road network, in this instance going from northern Mesopotamia to Damascus in Syria and then on as far as Egypt.

The economic basis of the empire was twofold: tribute (more politely called taxation) and enforced labor, corvée. Herodotus somehow got hold of a list of the empire's taxation districts which also doubled as military source units. He understood that there were twenty such, but Persian documents record anything from twenty to twenty-seven and perhaps the situation fluctuated over time. Tribute had to be paid either in kind or in coin; Darius was the first to strike a Persian coinage in both gold and silver, adorned with a symbolic image of himself as archer, and began the slow monetization of the empire. Sometimes the "kind" in which tribute had to be paid was, to a Greek, deeply shocking, as in the case of court eunuchs; or hugely thrilling, as in the case of the gold dust paid by "India" (in fact, only Sind and part of the Punjab). Monumental architecture at the vast palace complex at Persepolis begun by Darius in about 515 depicts tribute being paid, perhaps in connection with the annual New Year festival timed to coincide with the spring equinox (see Fig. 4.2). Numerous clay bureaucratic records also from Persepolis and a foundation inscription from Susa further give precious indications of the empire-wide sources of raw materials that went into the palaces' original construction, and of the huge and diverse labor force commandeered for that purpose.

Here is an excerpt from the Susa "Foundation Charter" (in a translation by M. Brosius 2000: doc. 45):

> The cedar timber was brought from a mountain called Lebanon. The Assyrian people brought it to Babylon. From Babylon the Carians and Ionians brought it to Susa. The sissoo-timber was brought from Gandara and from Carmania. The gold which was worked here was brought from Sardis and from Bactria. The precious stone lapis lazuli and carnelian which were worked here were brought from Sogdiana. The precious stone turquoise, which was brought here, that was brought from Chorasmia. The silver and the ebony were brought from Egypt . . .

And so on, and on, and on.

Empires tend to have an inbuilt dynamic that impels them to seek to expand. Sometimes, as in the case of the

Figure 4.2. The Great King of Persia (Darius I) enthroned at his palace of Persepolis, Iran, c. 515 BCE © The Trustees of the British Museum.

Romans, this is expressed in terms of a divinely appointed mission. In other cases, material greed, or the prestige of the emperor, or a genuine concern for the empire's security especially at the margins operate as the impulsive factor or factors. Darius's rule was no exception. Having quelled wide-scale unrest and dissidence in order to establish himself as emperor, and having initiated the construction of suitably palatial centers at Persepolis and Susa, he was in less than a decade on the aggressive march: starting from his northwest frontier that lay to the west of the Caspian Sea and proceeding as far west as the junction of Asia and Europe at the Bosporus strait within what is today western Turkey.

From the surviving written evidence, it is all too easy to look at the Persian empire through Greek eyes and to forget, as a result, that a more perennial threat to its stability was posed, not so much by the Greeks of the far west, but by the nomads of central Asia, around the Caspian and Aral seas. It was by a group of these, known to Herodotus as Massagetae, that Cyrus the Great had been killed in 530 or 529. The "Scythians," under which label these tribesmen all tended to be lumped together by Greeks and Persians alike, were endlessly unfinished business. However, Darius' Scythian campaign of 514–513 was by no means an unqualified success, and this was despite the support he was able to commandeer or cajole from a number of leading figures among his Greek subjects, men who governed their cities on Persia's behalf as "tyrants." The Greek *turannos* is possibly a loanword borrowed from the Lydian language of western Asia Minor, but from about 650 on such tyrants were quite a regular feature of Greek political life, and not only in Asiatic Greece by any means. However, for all their claim to rule their cities as sole autocrats, the Greek tyrants within the Persian empire normally remained firmly under the immediate control of a regional satrap or viceroy, who was often a member of the very extended Persian royal family. In light of his setback, therefore, Darius was by no means unwilling to find an excuse or reason to return to this far western theater, and in the 490s those same Asiatic Greeks provided him with a pretext that was more than just an excuse.

To the Persians, as to the Assyrians before them and the Hebrews after them, all Greeks were "Ionians," because that was the branch of the Greek people whom they first encountered, settled as they had been for hundreds of years along the Aegean coast of Asia. Chief among the Ionian Greek cities of the western Asiatic seaboard was Miletus, which had profited extensively from its marginal position between West and East both commercially and in intellectual terms. Thales, one of the Greek world's first known intellectuals, came from Miletus, a city which had a major hand in the foundation of many new Greek settlements around the Black Sea during his lifetime (around the turn of the seventh and sixth centuries BCE). A generation or two later, in the 540s, Miletus had found itself forcibly enrolled in Cyrus's new empire, obliged to renegotiate the favorable status it had enjoyed under the preceding Lydian empire of kings Alyattes and Croesus. In the late 520s, interestingly, Miletus had remained quiescent when many other imperial subjects, including those in Egypt and Babylonia, had sought to free themselves from Persian domination. In around 500 BCE, however, it had not merely joined in but actively promoted a rebellion that scholars refer to in shorthand as the Ionian Revolt.

Actually, that revolt involved other Greeks besides Ionians, and other non-Greek subjects, above all the colonists of the Phoenicians (of modern Lebanon) who uneasily shared the island of Cyprus with settlers from the Greek world. Nor was this revolt just a minor blip: it lasted for six whole annual campaigning seasons until it was finally crushed in the summer of 494, in a major naval battle fought not far from Miletus itself. The revolted Greek cities as a whole were treated perhaps with unpredictable leniency, but the ringleader Miletus was destroyed and its surviving inhabitants deported to the Persian Gulf. Moreover, a Persian task force under one of Darius' sons-in-law, the son of one of his closest advisers, was instructed to reassert Persia's interest in Europe on the far side of the Dardanelles ("Hellespont" to the Greeks), and he did so with such success that the northern coast of the Aegean became a vassal territory of the empire as far west as the fissiparous kingdom of Macedon. That Persian general was Mardonius, who was destined to breathe his last a decade and a half later in a corner of the foreign field of Plataea.

But Darius's eyes continued to rove after 492, and in 490 he entrusted a naval expedition to the joint command of a brother of his, Artaphernes, and a high-ranking Mede with special naval experience, Datis. The final objective of the expedition was left vague. But war aims included, at the least, revenge, restoration of prestige, enhanced security, and the delivery of a warning. Revenge was reserved for the two non-Asiatic Greek cities which had boldly but perhaps unwisely given material aid to the Ionians and others in revolt against Persia between 499 and 494: namely, Athens and Eretria (on the island of Euboea adjacent to Athens' territory of Attica). Eretria was duly flattened in an echo of the fate of Miletus, and many of its surviving inhabitants were likewise transported far away to the east of the Persian empire. But Athens—famously, notoriously—turned the tables on the aggressor and, with noteworthy help from its little ally Plataea, won the Battle of Marathon. That defeat in its turn became a major *casus belli* for Persia's next military intervention on the Greek mainland, in 480.

Or at least that was how it was seen from a dominant Greek point of view, that of the Athenians—whose view Herodotus was able to canvass and chose to represent a couple of generations later. Since we lack direct contemporary Persian testimony of any sort, official or unofficial, it may always be suggested that to the Great King seated in majesty upon his thrones at Susa and Persepolis in the Iranian south the faraway Greeks seemed as mere flies to wanton boys, or pinpricks on the hide of a rhinoceros. But my own view is that there was more to it than mere self-congratulatory Greek propaganda. Darius had not fared brilliantly in his one far northwestern expedition, in which Greek quisling rulers ("tyrants") had been intimately involved. Greeks were employed in the building of Darius' massive palaces toward the end of the sixth century, when his son Xerxes (not his eldest) was born. Xerxes himself will not have been utterly unacquainted with Greeks and Greek matters, nor utterly unmoved by a revolt that his own principal commander in 480, Mardonius, had been instrumental in putting down just four years before the Marathon debacle.

Marathon, whose 2500th anniversary was widely celebrated as well as commemorated in 2010/1, was for Greeks and Greece a truly remarkable and quite unpredictable success. Unfortunately, the only really usable ancient account comes from just the one source, Herodotus in the sixth book of his *Histories*; and there will always therefore remain large question marks over what exactly happened on the plain of Marathon in late summer 490 as well as over why the battle turned out the way it did. The expedition was commanded jointly by a brother of Darius, representing royal-family pride and honor, and by a Mede called Datis, who seems to have been something of a naval specialist. At any rate, the expedition was launched by sea ultimately from Phoenicia (modern Lebanon) and directly across the Aegean; this meant that the land troops and the cavalrymen and horses and all the materiel of battle had to be conveyed in special large transports, leaving little or no room for specialist men-of-war ships. After taking out Eretria on the western side of Euboea, the task force proceeded north to the large bay of Marathon, which was chosen as a landing-ground partly because of its convenient topography but also because of its political geography. In this area the aged (by then about 80?) Hippias, former tyrant of Athens, at least believed that he could count on a warm welcome and ancestral political support, and it was he who led the Persians' fleet to its safe anchorage and landing-ground.

But he, like the Persian high command as a whole, had reckoned without two factors: the fact that Athens since 508/7 had been a democracy (see further below) and so identified the possibility of Persian rule after military defeat with an intolerable enslavement to a despot; and, second, the military genius of a man who, having been himself a "tyrant" of the kind discussed above, ruling in the Persian interest in the Gallipoli peninsula region of the empire, on the European side of the Hellespont, had by now returned to his native Athens and accommodated himself somehow to the new democratic protocols of decision-making and military leadership. That returned and reformed native was Miltiades. As one of the ten elected Generals, it was his strategic and morale input that would generally be reckoned to have made the largest single contribution to the Athenian—and Plataean—victory at Marathon. Probably the 9,000 or so Athenians *plus* 1,000 or so Plataeans, who fought as heavy infantry hoplites in massed phalanx formation, were outnumbered by at least two to one. They apparently lacked the support of any, not just any competent, cavalry, whereas in a Persian army, the balance tended to go the other way: it was the cavalry that typically provided the punch and the panache, while the infantry was much more lightly armed than any Greek infantry and apparently fought first as bowmen and then as spearmen, in succession, in contrast to Greeks, who distinguished both archers from infantry and heavy-armed infantry—the crack force—from light infantry.

However, at Marathon, for some reason (Herodotus does not say, and moderns differ sharply among themselves) the Persians' cavalry either was not present at all at the decisive moment, or was present but made no substantial contribution to the outcome. Herodotus does not mention it at all. What does seem to have happened is that the Athenians and Plataeans guided by Miltiades spread themselves relatively thinly in the center of their line and bunched up on the wings. The thinned center then compensated for its smaller numbers by hurtling at a run, despite the heat and the weight of their arms and armor, into the enemy opposite, while the two wings ploughed through their opposite numbers and then rolled up the Persians' center from behind. If we are to believe

Herodotus, as many as 6,400 in round figures were killed on the Persian side, perhaps about 25 percent of the total; whereas a mere 192 (exactly) Athenians lost their lives (no figure is given for the Plataeans). The Athenian dead were treated as heroes—not merely in our generic sense of that word, but in the very specific cultural, that is religious, sense of the Greek word "hero." They were buried all together under a massive mound of earth and worshipped thereafter as semi-divine, more than merely mortal beings, functioning thereby as talismans and protectors of Athenians present and to come.

Marathon, at least in Greek and especially Athenian eyes, was thus a major triumph, and one to make as huge a song and dance about as was humanly possible (see further chapter 6). It would not have been surprising had the Persians felt a need to avenge this at least annoying defeat. But that was not the only cause for the Persians making war again directly on and in Greece ten years later. Security concerns dictated that control of the Aegean islands might be at least a desirable extra, and Persia's treatment of Miletus and Eretria served notice of what awful punishment any active military resistance to Persian royal power would entail. But, given what we know of Persian and indeed worldwide monarchical-imperial propaganda and self-image, the dented prestige suffered by Darius probably ranked very high among the Persians' motives, so that the shame of the Marathon defeat had to be expunged, with interest, if not by him (he died in 486), then by his son and successor, Xerxes, who besides had his own personal reasons for seeking a major, far-flung, prestige-bringing military campaign.

Revealingly, Xerxes was not Darius' oldest son and so not technically "crown prince"; undoubtedly his mother Atossa—by no means the last Persian Queen Mother to play politics—had an important hand in securing his accession, exploiting the fact that she was herself a daughter of the great Cyrus and that Xerxes had been (as the Byzantines would later put it) "born to the purple," that is, born after his father Darius' accession to the throne. The Persians, like many another eastern empire before and after them, chose to operate a royal harem system, and the inevitable outcome of that was a multiplicity of potential heirs. The conveniences of the system (such as manipulating and controlling the nobility) were thought to outweigh this one obvious disadvantage. Xerxes therefore had much to prove, not least his "right" to succeed an exceptionally potent father. Having first quelled major disturbances in Egypt and Babylonia, reminiscent of those that had troubled Darius' own accession, Xerxes seems to have made "Hellas" his number one enemy target. The invasion of 480 that he led in person was the culmination of a process of preparation beginning as far back as 484.

The empire did have a standing army, its core constituted by the elite royal force of 10,000 mainly Iranians known to the Greeks as the "Immortals." But for the Hellenic expedition of 480, as for say Darius' Scythian expedition of 513, that core had to be reinforced by conscripts drawn from every quarter of the empire and representing every conceivable type of armament. Such a force, inevitably, was not only unwieldy and complicated both to muster and to maneuver but also very hard to drill into any sort of cohesive unit or units, let alone to inspire with any degree of morale-boosting *esprit de corps*. Greek writers were probably prone to exaggerate the extent to which Persian commanders felt they had no choice but to rely on the whip to encourage their non-Persian soldiers into battle, but there was probably some fire to go with this propagandistic Greek smoke.

At sea, things were a good deal easier since the core of the Persian imperial navy for service in Mediterranean waters was provided by the Phoenicians of Tyre and Sidon and other cities in what is today Lebanon, backed up by Egyptians and Asiatic Greeks. And it is very noticeable how, after the much tougher naval showdown of 494, the expedition under Artaphernes and Datis in 490 had sliced through the Greek Aegean like a Persian *akinakês* (scimitar) through soft butter. But on land, in the plain of Marathon in eastern Attica, and lacking in action the cavalry that was normally such a key component of any Persian frontline force, the Persians as we have seen had been rocked back by the phalanx of hoplites (heavy infantrymen) of Athens and neighboring Plataea, suffering severe casualties as well as a major defeat. As things turned out, that defeat on land in pitched battle presaged the even more important one, eleven years later, at Plataea itself.

HELLAS

Invasions, especially a massive one like that led by emperor Xerxes in 480, tend, as Cicero put it, to "glue together" the forces of those whom they threaten. But that was true only up to a point of the Greeks' reaction to Xerxes. In a sense, there was no such thing as "Ancient Greece," at any rate no single political entity, let alone nation-state. Rather, Hellas (the Hellenes' own term—we call them "Greeks" and speak of "Greece," thanks to the Romans) was the sum of all those communities which identified themselves as Hellenic, which they would do, if pressed, on three main grounds: common language; shared descent; and common culture, especially in religious matters. Hellas in that sense at the time of the Graeco-Persian Wars stretched in modern terms from southern Spain in the West to Georgia in the Far East, from what they called the Pillars of Heracles (Gibraltar) to Phasis in Colchis. There were something on the order of 1,000 communities in all, together forming "Hellas," at any one time.

However, more often than not Greeks were divided from rather than united with each other, politically speaking, and often enough they were divided internally within their individual communities as well as divided between communities. Thus Spartans and Athenians (for example) tended to think of themselves as Spartans or Athenians first, and only secondarily as Greeks—except on the relatively rare occasions when they participated in events specifically as Hellenes, and that meant above all when they participated in designated pan-Hellenic (all and only Greek) events such as the major religious festivals of the Olympic Games and one or two others. But Spartans, who were on one level "Lacedaemonians" (inhabitants of the city-state of Lacedaemon or Sparta), distinguished themselves also as "Spartiates" from other, inferior "Lacedaemonians," who were not fully empowered citizens of the same territory; while Athenians might depending on the occasion want to think of themselves as "Eupatrids" (aristocrats) or as citizens of a particular "deme" (village, ward, parish) such as Acharnae rather than as "Athenians." In a culture thus fissile, getting Greeks to cooperate with each other as Greeks, even in the face of a massive non-Greek invasion threatening their very existence, was by no means easy—as is amply proved by the fact that only a little over 30 or so Greek communities out of a potential 700 or thereabouts actually managed to do so for any length of time during the Graeco-Persian Wars of 480–479.

In overall chronological perspective what is most striking about that cooperation is that it involved Sparta and Athens being—and fighting—on the same side. Both before and more especially after the Persian Wars they adopted the Greek default posture of intense rivalry, aggravated in their case not so much by geographical proximity and so direct competition for scarce economic resources but by fundamental cultural dissimilarity, even outright polar opposition. Both cities were in a sense the outcome of conquest, but whereas the Athenians, once united, boasted of being "autochthonous," that is of not having immigrated from elsewhere, the Spartans made no secret of the fact that their city had first come into being through immigration and had then been massively expanded by the conquest and enslavement of local populations who were no less Greek than they. Thus, whereas typically in the historical period slaves in Greek cities—of whom there were many thousands—were outsiders in the fullest sense (natally alienated, non-Greek foreigners), and usually bought and sold in slave-markets, the "slaves" of the Spartans (they used the common Greek term, *douloi*) suffered hereditary enslavement, being born into servitude communally as the descendants of people who had been conquered mainly in the eighth and seventh centuries. To add insult to injury, they were known, with brutal honesty but also degradingly, as "Helots," that is "captives," and they were in effect treated as such, as prisoners of war, permanently. The Athenians were no less keen than the Spartans on freedom as their birthright, and indeed evaluated their personal and political freedom in terms of the absence of the lifestyle restrictions imposed by servitude; but they did not find their own practice of chattel—or market-based—slavery at home to be incompatible with their democratic belief that the Spartans' sort of slave system was fundamentally illiberal and contrary to a properly Hellenic mode of slave management.

In terms of state-formation Sparta was both an early developer and a dyed-in-the-wool conservative society. The Spartans had already adopted the oddly mixed, mainly oligarchic form of political self-government with which they were operating in 480–479 at least a century earlier, whereas Athens had within living memory undergone a political transformation, indeed revolution, that gave the world its first taste and expression of democracy, "people-power." To most Spartans most of the time, Athenian-style democracy—direct, open, participatory government by means of votes at mass meetings, each citizen counting for one and no one for more than one—was anathema. It was a system they never sought to introduce at home and which they fervently attempted to resist or overthrow abroad, not least within their own military alliance. They had many objections, but, above all, Athenian-style democracy was to them unacceptably undisciplined. It thus fundamentally contradicted their own hierarchical, top-down, military-minded worldview, and was deeply at odds with the continued existence in Sparta of not just an old-world aristocracy but even a unique hereditary dual kingship.

Consistently, the disciplinarian Spartans were also the first—indeed, for centuries the only—Greek city to devise and impose a centrally organized and controlled system for educating their male (and, to a smaller extent, their female) young in the dominant values of the adult community. This was education of a military cast, both practically and symbolically. However, it should not be inferred from this that the Spartans were therefore in a negative sense militaristic, always spoiling for a fight, on inappropriate or inadequate grounds; at least, that was not the case as regards any external enemy, Greek or non-Greek, at any rate not after 550 BCE or so. Rather, their educational system of communal socialization was devised primarily to ensure the internal harmony and cohesion and the automatic feeling for cooperation that were necessary to enable them to cope with the threat constantly posed by the enemy within, the Helots. Non-Spartans too often failed to realize just what a constraint this eternal, homegrown factor of a many times larger and by no means entirely reconciled subject population placed on all Spartan foreign as well as domestic policy. Sometimes, but only very rarely, the threat was translated into open Helot revolt, as in 464. It was to guard against that eventuality that in 421, when the Spartans and Athenians made a separate peace treaty, the Spartans insisted on inserting a very striking clause, unreciprocated on the Athenians' side, compelling the Athenians to come to their aid "if the slave class should revolt."

Athens by contrast went through a more normal pattern of political and social evolution—from a collection of villages to a coherent state, and from unquestioned aristocratic domination (both political and economical as well as religious) to a more open and moderate form of oligarchy, in which power resided chiefly in the hands of those wealthy enough not to have to work for a living themselves and to be able to command the unfree labor required to do the mainly agricultural work for them. The really big political changes, however, which were destined to set Athens apart from all other Greek cities except Sparta as a "major league" player, came during the sixth century. First, there were the moderately oligarchic reforms ushered in by Solon; then there was a lengthy period of relatively benevolent and culturally enlightened despotism by Peisistratus and his son Hippias; and finally, climactically—a plague on both their houses—there erupted a popular revolt against both oligarchy and tyranny that eventuated in the emergence before 500 BCE of a primitive but specially dynamic form of democracy. It was with this newfangled political regime that Athens won the Battle of Marathon in 490, the credit for that being due chiefly to the citizens who belonged in the top 30 or so percent economic bracket. Then came the Battle of Salamis in 480, for which the credit went rather to the bottom 50 percent of citizens, who rowed the new trireme warships; this was achieved thanks to the Athenians' collective possession of a unique form of national wealth in the form of productive silver mines, and it was decisively shaped by the strategic genius of one exceptionally farsighted politician, Themistocles. Sparta, by contrast, fought at Plataea the following year in the time-honored hoplite military way, under the time-honored—and increasingly outmoded—direction of a man chosen to command solely because of his royal birth.

After Sparta and Athens came what has sometimes been labeled the "third" Greece, the more standard, generally more conventional mass of Greek cities, most of which were relatively very small and quite insignificant. It has been estimated that the modal (most frequently occurring) size of the adult male citizen body of a "normal" Greek polis fell in the range of 500 to 2,000. To them of course must be added minor males and females of all ages, together with free and unfree noncitizens, so that for instance a figure of 500 adult male citizens might be enlarged to comprise some 2,000 persons of citizen status both male and female, to which could be added a like figure of free and unfree noncitizens combined. Within this third tier there were exceptions—there are always exceptions: for instance, Corinth. Corinth had a very modest home territory of only some 90 square kilometers, but it punched well above the weight that could have been predicted from that size of territory alone because of its geopolitical situation. Strategically located across the isthmus linking the Peloponnese to central Greece, it lay between Sparta and Athens, and it cleverly exploited its intermediate situation. It was blessed moreover with harbors on either side of the isthmus, on respectively the Corinthian and Saronic Gulfs. It was a born magnet for trade between eastern (Aegean) and western (central Mediterranean) commerce. It entered very early on into the favorite Greek pastime of "colonization"—as the process of establishing new settlements almost all round the Mediterranean and Black Sea is known in the standard scholarly literature, though this is rather misleading, since in fact most of the new "colonial" foundations were from the start politically independent cities. The literal translation of the Greek term *apoikia* as "home-from-home" or "settlement abroad" is therefore often a better rendering than "colony," which may carry misleading associations of British nineteenth-century imperialism. Corinth's major overseas foundations were Kerkyra, in Latin Corcyra (modern Corfu), and Syracuse in Sicily, both founded in the third quarter of the eighth century. Relations between "colony" and "mother-city," being symbolic and ultimately religious, were typically friendly, though as it happens Kerkyra and Corinth did not always get on brilliantly. Corinth, together with the island state of Aegina lying not very far away in the Saronic Gulf, were—after Sparta and Athens—the most important members of the loyalist anti-Persian alliance in 480–479.

However, the vast majority of Greek cities were not fighting against the Persians. Some of these tried to stay out of the fighting altogether, and remain neutral, watching the outcome from the sidelines as it were. But a very large number actively fought on the Persian side, some admittedly under coercion—they were then subjects of that empire, indeed quite recently re-subjected after revolt—but many, too many one might think, from choice: either because they felt sure the Persians would win and wanted to be on the winning side, or because a Greek enemy of theirs was taking the opposite, loyalist side. Conversely, in the case of the Phocians of central mainland Greece, we are solemnly assured by Herodotus that these Greeks opted for loyalism solely because their Greek neighbors and enemies in Thessaly had "medized," gone over to Persia. Whatever may have been the actual truth in individual instances, even a cursory scrutiny of the contingents lined up on either side is sufficient to dispel for ever such overfamiliar, oversimplistic assertions as that "the Greeks" defeated "the Persians" in the "Persian Wars."

5

THE FACE OF THE BATTLE
OF PLATAEA

the most splendid victory of all those about which
we have knowledge

—Herodotus

In the two climactic years of the Persian invasion of Greece five main battles were fought: two on land (Thermopylae 480, Plataea 479), two at sea (Artemisium 480, Salamis 480), and one amphibious (Mycale 479); four in "mainland" Greece, one (Mycale) on and off the coast of Asia (Minor). Thermopylae and Salamis are far and away the most celebrated of them, and the most written about. Plataea, indeed, could almost be called the great unknown battle in one of the great wars of history. One reason for Plataea's relative lack of celebrity, as already noted, is that it was essentially a Spartan (and Peloponnesian), not Athenian, victory, and the Athenians have been far more vocal, far more influential over the surviving tradition of the Wars, than the Spartans (chapter 6). Another is that Plataea was a small state—in the shadow first of Thebes, then of Athens, and physically destroyed more than once, first by the Persians in 480, then by the Spartans in 426, then again by the Thebans in 373. It did come into its own later, as the site of an annual commemoration of the Persian Wars, a freedom festival (Eleutheria). But that was at a time well after 300 BCE, and by then individual Greek city-states had lost any genuine autonomy and formed part of large territorial kingdoms, such as the one ruled from Macedon by the Antigonids (a successor dynasty to that of Philip II and Alexander the Great). These kingdoms were in turn superseded by the greatest ancient empire of them all, that of Rome. Yet a third reason for the battle's lack of its due meed of celebrity is more technical, and due to the nature of the surviving evidence for it. Herodotus' account is not just the best that we have, but really the only usable one—in the sense that the others are more or less derivative from it rather than independently grounded and valuable. Yet Herodotus' is both quite brief and lacunose, leaving a number of puzzles hanging. By that I don't mean to imply that it is surprisingly poor. As Noah Whatley long ago pointed out (1964), there are very good reasons why no battle before a relatively modern era—not just no ancient Greek battle—is very well documented. That is also one, if only one, explanation for the large variability in modern attempted reconstructions of it too. But before we add our own, we must first briefly set the military scene.

Figure 5.1. An Athenian lady with her oriental servant surmounts the molded head of a bearded Persian warrior; Attic red-figure jug c. 410–400, from Nola, Italy, now British Museum. © The Trustees of the British Museum.

PAUL CARTLEDGE

90

Xerxes, unlike his aging and possibly physically failing father Darius ten years before (see Fig. 4.2), had elected to serve and command in person against Hellas, as he led or drove his massive land army from its western muster-point, Sardis in Lydia, across the strait known to the Greeks as the Hellespont in spring 480. Greeks had long had wind of his eventual invasion, some four years' notice in all. This duration of preparation was by no means untypical for a multiregional, multinational Persian force and was partly a simple reflection of the empire's complicated and vastly extended geography. But the length of time involved might reasonably be hoped also to have the effect of sapping an enemy's morale in advance.

Xerxes was in direct contact with and control of his land army, but this campaign was, as it had to be, a combined amphibious, land-and-sea operation. The principal component of the Persians' Mediterranean navy was as usual supplied by Phoenicians, both those of the Asiatic mainland (modern Lebanon) and those of Cyprus, an island divided then as now between rival ethnic and political groups. Herodotus' figures for the original Persian forces must be wildly exaggerated; he estimated the land forces in 480 at over 3 million men, the naval contingents at some quarter of a million (crewing over 1,200 three-banked warships). Soberer modern estimates cut down the land component to between 100,000 and 200,000, and the fleet by perhaps a half, but even so this was a simply massive force, not exceeded until the allied D-Day operation of 1944 in the Second World War. In 479, of course, after Xerxes' return to Persia with the remainder of the fleet after the defeat at Salamis, what was left of the infantry/cavalry "mopping-up" forces—300,000, according to Herodotus—may in fact have amounted to no more than about 70,000 to 100,000, placing them on roughly the same numerical plane as the forces mustered on the loyalist Greek side.

And, let it not be forgotten, many of the 200,000 to 400,000 on the Persian side were Greeks, the majority of them Persia's existing Greek subjects. Among these a significant minority were mercenaries, for which category of fighter the Greeks had two words, one meaning "foreigners" or "strangers" (*xenoi*), the other "helpers" (*epikouroi*). Neither of those terms captures the precisely mercenary element in their hired or bought status, which perhaps reflects the fact that serving as a mercenary in ancient Greece bore some of the negative stigma that it has in some other societies and periods—and had therefore to be disguised by euphemism. At any rate, there were an awful lot of mercenaries about in fifth-century Greece—and had been since at least the seventh and earlier sixth centuries, when creating a portable and concealable means to pay them may have been one of the major stimuli towards the production of coinages in electrum, gold, and silver by the Greek cities from about 600 BCE on.

The most famous group of mercenaries in Greek history are those immortalized by one of their number, Xenophon's "Ten Thousand." Actually, there were about 13,000 of them when they set off in 401 under the leadership of a Persian princely pretender to try to take the throne for their paymaster from his elder brother, Artaxerxes II. But by the end, in 400, as they wended their way back from deepest Babylonia (southern Iraq today) to Greek civilization at Byzantium after surviving a series of hair-raising and foot-pulverizing adventures, they did indeed number around 10,000. They were thus a quite huge force, several Greek citizen-bodies' worth, in themselves; but no less important a consideration was that more than half of them had signed up from impoverished Arcadia and Achaea in the Peloponnese. It is no coincidence that the one place of regional origin mentioned for Greek mercenaries who signed up under Artaxerxes' predecessor Xerxes was again Arcadia; poverty rather than pro-Persian or anti-Greek principle was very likely the main motive driving them into the Persian camp.

Aware of the impending invasion, perhaps in the early summer of 481, a small but significant number of mainland Greek cities had sent delegates to the sacred and strategically pivotal Isthmus of Corinth. Here within the sanctuary dedicated to sea-god and earthquake-god Poseidon they swore the first Greek oaths of military significance that Herodotus chose to record—oaths of alliance. They thereby formed themselves into what moderns rather grandly call "the Hellenic League." Certainly it was Hellenic, literally so: the allies called themselves simply but resonantly "the Greeks" (*hoi Hellênes*), and in total numbers of armed forces they could in theory have come quite close to matching those of their invaders. But unity of name did not translate easily or precisely into unity of purpose and action. This was partly because of a radical mismatch already noted between the two leading mainland Greek powers respectively by land and by sea, Sparta and Athens. Given that the Hellenic resistance had to be no less amphibious than the Persian assault, closely coordinated combined land-sea operations were not just desirable but indispensable. No one doubted that, Athens' feat at Marathon notwithstanding, Sparta was the leading military power in land warfare, both alone and as head of a mainly Peloponnesian alliance that constituted an overall majority of the allied Hellenic cities. But how—indeed, why—should Sparta also have overall command of the naval forces, the vast majority of which would be contributed by Athens? Yet, such was the traditional authority of Sparta in the military sphere, and such the desire to avoid the deficits of a divided command, that Sparta was in fact awarded the overall leadership of the alliance by sea as well as by land. It is often easy to forget that the commander-in-chief of the Hellenes at the emphatically naval battle of Salamis was a Spartan.

However, the Hellenic allies' very first joint action was anything but joint. Not being in a position to resist the Persians at their point of crossing from Asia to Europe, they contemplated where their first practicable line of defense might be. What they required above all was a defensible location that would minimize the Persians' seeming numerical superiority. So they settled initially and with typical lack of adequate advance intelligence on the pass of Tempe that led from Persian-dominated Macedonia into Persian-leaning Thessaly. In fact, the loyalist allies actually sent a force of troops up north from their central Greek command center (such as it was), only to discover—as they should surely already have known—that Tempe could be too easily turned for it to be worth their making even a token show of resistance there.

The case was rather different for their second choice, the pass known (thanks to its sulfur springs) as Thermopylae or the "hot gates." This kilometer-long, east-west pass hard up against the Maliac Gulf was far tougher to turn, at any rate for an army the size of Xerxes', and far easier for a relatively small force quickly to make defensible; indeed, the local Phocians had already enhanced its defensibility with a fortification at the narrowest point, known as the Middle Gate. Besides, Thermopylae offered a good line of communication to the Greek fleet positioned on the northern end of the very long island of Euboea. Yet even so the Spartans, the overall leaders of the resisting Greeks, seemed themselves to be in at least two minds as to the wisdom of a Thermopylae defense. On the one hand, the senior of their two kings, Leonidas, was apparently in no doubt whatsoever, and did all he could both strategically and ideologically to ensure a good turnout of Greek allies at the pass. But his city seems not to have striven very energetically to back him. Out of the total force of some 6,000 to 7,000 eventually mustered under his command at the pass, perhaps fewer than a thousand came from Sparta—and they included only 300 picked Spartiates besides Leonidas himself. At any rate, that is the one figure that "everyone knows," based as it is ultimately on Herodotus. A later, generally inferior source speaks rather of 1,000 "Lacedaemonians," a figure that could include, as well as the elite 300, both Helot light-armed auxiliaries and free hoplites drawn from the subordinate communities of Laconia and Messenia; the latter were known as Perioeci or "Outdwellers," and there were upwards of 50 such communities, mostly in Laconia (southeast Peloponnese). But even so, 1,000 was still a rather paltry contribution on the face of it.

It was, however, claimed—and this was clearly the official Spartan line, which in public at least Leonidas had to endorse—that a larger force would arrive in due course, and good reasons of a religious nature were alleged for its arrival being necessarily later than that of the supposed advance guard. All the same, it has to be said, Leonidas found himself dangerously and in fact fatally exposed. Soon after arriving in the pass and refortifying its middle section, if not already before, he had been told of a narrow, winding, and difficult pass across the mountains behind him, that is to his south, and he accordingly posted a force of 1,000 local Phocian Greeks to guard it. However, thanks partly to these Phocians' incompetence, and partly to a notorious act of treachery by another local Greek (from the Malian people), his position in the pass was ultimately rendered untenable. Ephialtes, the Malian in question, is known to fame, or rather infamy, in Greece today because his name serves as the equivalent of our word "nightmare." Famously, Leonidas and all but two of his 300 Spartiates perished at Thermopylae, in a consciously chosen do-or-die defense, along with the 700 magnificent troops sent by the little Boeotian town of Thespiae. (Happily, the Thespians' gallantry is today commemorated, alongside the Spartans', at roughly the site of the final engagement.)

The campaign, though a failure (Herodotus calls it a "trauma" or wound) in straightforward military terms, did at all events have the three surely desired effects of, first, inflicting a serious blow upon Xerxes' forces (casualties perhaps reached as high as 20,000), not least upon their morale, second, holding up their advance southward in order to gain extra time for the

Athenians and others to muster their naval forces, and, third and most important of all perhaps, maintaining connection with a fleet that, thanks in part to some timely gales, did far better than expected against the mainly Phoenician ships of the Persians. Artemisium, the fleet's base, wasn't a city or even a town; the name refers to a sanctuary devoted to Artemis located at the northern tip of the island of Euboea. Here the Greek loyalist fleet had hunkered down, in considerable trepidation, awaiting the arrival of the far larger and better trained Persian fleet. It had made a stately progress from the Hellespont, passing through rather than round the Mt. Athos prong of the Chalcidice peninsula, thanks to a spectacular and still visible feat of Persian engineering. At first, all went well for the Persians as they encountered the fearful Greeks, but then the tables or rather the wind turned against them, and a very large number of Persian ships was irreparably wrecked. This both evened up the numbers and, above all, gave the defending Greeks a great morale boost, as they—in a cultural reaction second nature to them—attributed the wind's destructiveness to the action of a kindly god, Boreas, responding they imagined as only he knew how to their solicitous worship of him. So, although Thermopylae was in the end a heavy defeat for the resisting Greeks, it could have turned out very much worse; and the twin campaign of Thermopylae-Artemisium somehow paved the way for the next major encounter in 480, the result of which went entirely the other way.

After proceeding triumphantly through the Thermopylae pass, the Persian forces first sacked the two Boeotian cities that had refused to surrender to them, Plataea and Thespiae, and then occupied and likewise sacked and ransacked the much bigger prize of Athens, including—especially—the buildings and artifacts that adorned the sacred Acropolis. The Athenians themselves, however, had mostly already evacuated their city and taken up defensive positions to the south, on the islet of Salamis (an integral part of the Athenian state), while sending their noncombatants and livestock to relatively safe havens on Euboea and in the Peloponnese. (A much later document, of very doubtful authenticity, known as the "Themistocles Decree," maintains stoutly that this evacuation was all carefully planned well in advance.) At about the time of the autumnal equinox, almost four weeks after the combined Thermopylae-Artemisium operations, Xerxes' navy went down to a resounding and stunning defeat in the narrow strait by Salamis. It has often been found puzzling that Xerxes should, by deciding to fight here, have nullified in advance his great advantage in numbers of ships and quality of seamanship, and the Greeks themselves liked to attribute his rash decision to enter the narrow channel with his whole armada of perhaps 600 ships to the superior cunning and downright trickery of the equivalent of Marathon's Miltiades—the canny Themistocles. However, another less glamorous explanation might be that Xerxes felt he needed to win one crushing face-to-face encounter at sea in the Athenians' backyard rather than landing first in the Peloponnese and executing a stealthier but lengthier and less heroic series of maneuvers by land and sea combined.

As it was, therefore, something over 300 allied Greek ships managed to lure or at any rate corral a larger, professionally superior Persian fleet within the sort of confined space where the latter's natural and learned advantages were effectively rendered null. Other loyalist Greek cities contributed mightily, the island state of Aegina and the twin-harbor state of Corinth to the fore; even little and landlocked Plataea heroically contributed its share of oarsmen. But the Greek victory was essentially due to the Athenians' 180 to 200 ships, the efficacy of which was owed to a largely unpredictable combination of factors. There had been an exceptionally lucky strike of silver in the state-owned mines just two years before, and the democratic Athenians were persuaded by the rhetoric of the brilliantly foresighted and improvisatory Themistocles, against their initial more mercenary inclinations, to devote this handy surplus to the construction of a 200-strong fleet of trireme warships. The three-banked, 170-oared trireme had been the ship-of-the-line in the most advanced Greek naval warfare for over forty years by then, but still many Greek states lagged in adopting it, simply because it was such an expensive and risky investment: it cost about 1 talent—or 6,000 days of a skilled craftsman's labor—to build, and could be permanently disabled with just one piercing thrust below the waterline by an enemy ship's bronze-sheathed ram. The Athenians in 483/2, inspired by Themistocles, took the plunge, and in 480 Athenian oarsmen and supernumerary crew passed over from being naval nonentities to the status of naval heroes in a trice.

So major indeed was the impact of the Salamis victory, and so successful were the Athenians in trumpeting it, that even the normally sober Herodotus was convinced that it was the most decisive battle of the entire Graeco-Persian Wars, prompting him to dub the Athenians "the saviours of Hellas"

(7.139). But, if so, we must resolutely ask of him, how come Salamis did not end the war? Why did Plataea have to be fought? And what if Plataea had been lost—where would the Salamis victory have left the Greeks then? Of course, had Salamis been lost, then there would have been no Plataea—but that's another matter altogether.

The import and impact of Salamis cannot, however, be gainsaid. It was a major humiliation for Xerxes personally, who had watched the conflict from the Attic shore and chose to return to Asia immediately afterwards, and it was a key turning point in the campaign. But it was by no means the end of the Persians' Greek affair, and when Xerxes departed, he might reasonably have had every confidence that the man to whom he handed over the supreme command would be able to finish the job satisfactorily. That man was Mardonius, son of an intimate companion of Xerxes' father Darius, a general with a proven track record of success in the Aegean sphere, and not improbably—as Herodotus represents him—one of the prime movers behind the expedition as such, along with Great King Xerxes himself. And there is a good case for claiming that Mardonius ought to have finished the job, especially as Plataea was as near-run a thing as Waterloo, on the razor's edge, as the Greeks themselves might have put it—at least, that is what my reading of Herodotus' admittedly less than wholly impeccable account suggests to me.

In the unadorned words of Herodotus (9.62.2) Plataea was "a fierce battle that went on for a long time." More poetically, the Athenian tragic playwright Aeschylus, who had himself fought at Marathon and possibly also Salamis, had characterized the entire Graeco-Persian Wars in his tragic drama *Persians* of 472 as a contest of Greek spear against Asiatic bow (lines 85–6, 146–8, 239–40). Actually, more arms than just spears and bows were involved on either side, but that will do well enough as a summary, so long as it's remembered that spears and bows could be wielded by horsemen as well as infantrymen. Moreover, the maneuvers antecedent to the actual engagement, or rather engagements, can sometimes seem as interesting as the battle—or sequence of engagements—itself. But let it be said again loud and clear: we shall never be able with total confidence to recapture "what actually happened" in the critical months of August–September 479, culminating in the Battle (or battles . . .) of Plataea.

Mardonius it has been argued should not have retired from Attica for the winter of 480/79—though, if he had not, he surely would soon have encountered severe supply problems. As it was, he did withdraw, northward, to the comparative safety and security of Thessaly, one of mainland Greece's breadbaskets. From there he was extremely active on the diplomatic front, in ways that showed he was being well advised on the state of Greek customs and sensitivities as well as on the eternally fragile nature of Greek interstate relations. A telling moment came when allegedly on the orders of Xerxes himself Alexander I, the vassal king of the Macedonians, was sent to Athens as a top-level diplomatic emissary offering various bribes to wean the Athenians away from their Hellenic alliance. The Spartans, fearing perhaps the effects of the "my enemy's enemy is my friend" syndrome, sent a counter-embassy to stymie him. The Athenians themselves, in Herodotus's highly favorable account, did not bat an eyelid but, stoutly maintaining that their loyalty should never for a second have been doubted by the Spartans, seized the opportunity to deliver to their allies and co-leaders a magnificently patriotic and liberationist Hellenic harangue, and to Alexander a blunt rebuff.

This is indeed the earliest of the expressions of a "Hellenic" identity known to posterity, and since they remained as rare as hen's teeth it's worth briefly pausing to see in what terms Herodotus at least, himself a Greek from a mixed Greek-Asiatic background, thought a Hellenic patriot ought to identify Greekness. First in temporal order, and in evaluative priority, according to Herodotus' "Athenians," came a common overriding religious obligation: the images and temples of the gods that the Persians had torched had to be avenged. Second, there was the shared fact of being Greek as a result of consanguinity and linguistic identity: Greeks were Greeks because of common "blood" and common "tongue." Third—religion again to the fore—the Athenians invoked common Greek "customs," both religious and secular: that is, worshipping the same gods in the same way, above all through the practice of animal blood sacrifice, and enjoying a shared way of life, that is, importantly, not practicing such customs as polygamy or anthropophagy that allegedly besmirched and demeaned the systems of "barbarians." Whether in fact it was a relatively abstract notion of Hellenism that determined the Athenians not to go over to the Persian side, or rather more concrete concerns for the liberty of the citizen, may be doubted. At all events, the coming of the spring and summer of 479 saw "the Hellenes" still as united (or not) as they had been at the end of the preceding summer and autumn of 480.

In June 479, having stocked up on freshly harvested Thessalian grain and other supplies, Mardonius moved his forces south, forcing again the evacuation of Athens; and once again he both occupied all Attica and dealt further destruction to the chief city's holiest places. Yet still the Spartans delayed marching north to oppose force with force. Why? "The rigid closeness of that oligarchic government [Sparta] kept . . . its motives and its policy no less a secret to contemporaneous nations than to modern inquirers" was well said in 1837 by Edward Bulwer Lytton, echoing Thucydides' famous comment (5.68) on the "secrecy of the Spartan regime" in the context of the Atheno-Spartan Peloponnesian War some six decades later. But it has to be said that Herodotus' account of 479 does not go out of its way to enlighten the gloom; indeed, it reveals all too clearly the contradictory nature of his Greek sources. On the one hand, there were those informants who told Herodotus that the Spartans had never really intended to fight the Persians north of the Isthmus of Corinth in any event, and that that was why they allegedly spent more time and energy in trying to build a wall across the Isthmus than in preparing to send significant forces north of it. On the other hand, Herodotus does also seem to have accepted that the Spartans were indeed genuinely an extraordinarily pious people and so given credence to their own claim that it was one of their major annual religious festivals—the Hyacinthia, held annually in high summer in honor of Apollo and Hyacinthus—that had prevented their marching out until after it had been duly celebrated.

However, more robust modern criticism justly points out that the Spartans could have marched out before the Hyacinthia if they had really wanted to and seeks an explanation for their delay in doing so, rather, in the general mood of defeatism of the other Peloponnesians (which could also account for some of the seeming oddity of the Spartan commander's behavior once he had come within range of the Persian forces in Boeotia). Alternatively, the delay could simply have reflected the time it took to prepare for an expedition of such an unprecedented scale and not have been due only to a need for reassurance that the Isthmus fortification wall was well and truly finished before they ventured north of it. At all events, when they did eventually march out, allegedly tricking yet another Athenian embassy to Sparta that demanded instant action, it was in full force but at dead of night—a circumstance for which Spartan soldiers were specifically trained. The subterfuge could equally plausibly be explained by a desire to cause maximum surprise, not principally to the detriment of the Athenians but so as to allow the least possible latitude to any allied resistance from among their Peloponnesian allies—or enemies.

It was at Eleusis in Attica to the west of the city of Athens that the Peloponnesian forces under Regent Pausanias (deputizing for the under-age Pleistarchos, son of Leonidas) joined up with the Athenian troops under Aristeides. It is also there and then, as noted earlier, that those commentators who wish to give a historical context to the swearing of a genuine, authentic Plataea Oath imagine that it could have been administered. Certainly, the surroundings would have been auspicious. Eleusis was the home of one of the few genuinely Panhellenic religious institutions, the Mysteries or secret rituals held twice a year in honor of "The Two Goddesses," that is, universal earth mother goddess Demeter and her daughter, known variously as simply "Daughter" (Kore), or as Persephone, or in local Athenian dialect as Pherephatta. Thus Eleusis was both a township within the territory of the Athenian state (a "deme" like Acharnae: chapter 2) and a sacred space that was open to all Greeks but yet fiercely overseen and controlled by the central authorities of the Athenian city, which was by now a democratic city. Anyone who could speak Greek well enough, even foreign-born, non-Greek slaves, could be initiated into the secret mysteries of Eleusis on an individual basis. Almost all Athenians it seems did choose to be, especially in the hopes of a better or at least less painful afterlife. Keeping the two goddesses happy by worshipping them assiduously was also thought to be a way of ensuring the blessings of agricultural increase in this life too. Whether or not an Oath of Plataea was now sworn at Eleusis will never be known for sure, but the odds—if my arguments in chapter 2 are at all cogent—are surely against it.

From Eleusis the Greek allies marched north to Boeotia, where Mardonius had withdrawn after, as mentioned, occupying and again destroying Athens itself in June. He made his camp and fortified it on the north bank of the Asopos river, which was to be a key player as well as a clear topographical marker in the conflict to come. Against him Pausanias took up his position on the high ground to the south of the river, having traversed the passes of Mount Kithairon and settled near the ruined site of ancient Plataea (already destroyed once by the Persians, as it was to be later by the Spartans and the Thebans). The strategy of Mardonius was therefore to lure the Greeks down into the plain to make them more vulnerable to his superior cavalry. At the same time, he sought to play on the undisguisable dissension among the nervous allied Greek ranks.

Under the Spartans' and so Pausanias' overall command were the following: Peloponnesians—from Tegea, other Arcadian communities, Corinth, Sicyon, Epidaurus, Troezen, Lepreon, Phleious, Mycenae, Tiryns, and Hermion; central Greek mainlanders—from Athens, Megara, Plataea, and Ambracia; northern Greeks—from Poteidaia; and islanders both eastern and western—from Eretria, Chalcis, Aegina, Cephallenia, and Leucas. According to Herodotus (but his are probably just "paper" figures, conveniently rounded, for the most part), the total of heavy infantrymen was of the order of 40,000 men, reinforced perhaps by a similar number of light- or lighter-armed. The largest contingent by far was that provided by Sparta—5,000 full citizens, and a like number of heavy infantry from the free but politically subordinate communities of Laconia and Messenia. An enduring puzzle is the number given by Herodotus for the Helots, no fewer than seven for each Spartiate or 35,000 in all. Possibly some of these were indeed equipped and did actually fight as light-armed troops (*psiloi*), but the majority surely were intended to and did function as orderlies, or as communications and commissariat operatives—if indeed as many as 35,000 were in fact dispatched to Plataea, rather than 7:1 being an estimate of the ratio of the total number of adult male Helots to the adult male Spartans of fighting age.

Against them, under Mardonius, were arrayed cavalry and infantry, both non-Greek and Greek, significantly less well armored on the whole. Herodotus itemizes no fewer than 45 peoples under Xerxes' original command in 480, but of these only five are featured in his account of the Plataea battle. Again, it should be recalled that of his original supposedly 3 million a mere tenth or 300,000 were envisaged by him as still active under Mardonius in mainland Greece in 479—though both figures are surely vastly exaggerated. Numbers are impossible to determine with any precision, but conceivably Mardonius had at least 70,000 and possibly as many as 100,000 men under his command. The cavalry forces were not dissimilar to those later deployed at the battle of Cunaxa near Babylon in 401, suggesting that in this as in other respects Persian armies tended to operate to a traditional model, regardless of particular successes or, as in this case, failure. The Scythians (Sacae to Herodotus, a subgroup of this large and fierce circum-Caspian Sea people) were said to be the best of them, and probably were among those later to be found attacking the Spartans. There were also Bactrians (from modern Afghanistan) and Indians, stationed to the right of the Medes. The crack infantry were as usual the Persian "Immortals" (see Fig. 5.2).

Of the Greeks fighting with and for Persia the most significant contribution by far was that made by the hoplites and cavalrymen of Boeotian Thebes; their "medism" was seemingly unforced and remained saliently controversial for 150 years and more thereafter. But though extreme, their decision

Figure 5.2. The "Immortals," as the Greeks knew a Persian King's elite guard on campaign, depicted on glazed bricks from the Palace of Susa, Iran. Erich Lessing/Art Resource, NY.

actively to favor the Persians over their fellow Greeks was by no means unique. Loyalty to one's own *polis* rather than to any wider patriotic concept of "Hellas" was the norm at most points in most eras of Greek history. Quite consistently with that, a recently discovered early fifth-century inscription has been interpreted to show that the Thebans had seized the moment of the Persian invasion to occupy and control for themselves key places on the neighboring island of Euboea, which had remained by and large loyal to the anti-Persian Greek cause (not altogether surprisingly, in view of the destruction wreaked on Euboean Eretria in 490). If that dating and interpretation are correct, the opprobrium subsequently heaped on the Thebans by their enemies from the Athenians to Alexander the Great need excite little wonder. What is truly wonderful—as Herodotus amply recognized—is that for at least a couple of campaigning seasons sufficient numbers of key Greek cities did pull adequately together, on broadly "Hellenic" loyalist grounds.

After some initial skirmishes, which the loyalist Greeks won on points—thanks largely to the killing of a statuesque Persian cavalry commander (see below for details)—a stalemate soon ensued. Insofar as the allies may be said to have been deployed in a regular line, the Spartans and the Tegeans (the most important of their allies in Arcadia) occupied a ridge on the far right—which was considered the position of honor in any Greek heavy-infantry phalanx. The Athenians were granted the next most honorific station, the far left-hand position, on a hillock, though in order to secure it they allegedly had first to win an ideological dispute against the Spartans' Peloponnesian ally Tegea in which both sides bandied rival claims to glorious achievement often in their dim and distant, largely or wholly mythical past. But the Athenians did have one exceptionally salient and very recent achievement to boast of and appeal to: their stunning victory at Marathon, a mere eleven years earlier. Herodotus reports that the decision between the two was made by "the whole force of the Spartans" by means of shouting—an authentic touch, since that was indeed the way that they made their political and electoral decisions in their assemblies back home in Sparta (Thucydides 1.87), much to the surprise of other Greeks who voted either by raising their right hands (*kheirotonia*) or by casting a ballot—usually a pebble (*psêphos*), whence our technical term "psephology."

Between the Spartans and the Athenians were stationed, going from right to left, the Corinthians, other Peloponnesians, and so on up until the 600 Plataeans stationed next to the Athenians. I have spoken of a "Greek heavy-infantry phalanx," but it should in fairness be made clear that scholars are in considerable disagreement as to just how heavy it would have been in 479, that is, just what weight of arms and armor a typical Greek hoplite of this period would have borne. For example, would his corselet (breastplate) still have been of bronze, as had regularly been the case since from as early as 700 BCE (and as I'd imagine that of at least the full Spartan citizen hoplites still was), or rather of the lighter—and cheaper—stiffened linen material that became widely prevalent in the fifth century? How heavy would his basically wooden shield have been, given that it would have been (out of necessity) a meter or so wide? (See Figs. 5.3 and 5.4.)

Older estimates usually reckon the total weight of all that equipment at something on the order of 50 to 70 pounds (20–30 kilograms), but revisionist estimates would now diminish that by a third, perhaps even a half. In the broiling summer sun

Figure 5.3. Small bronze figurine, 6th-century BCE, depicting a Spartan commander, possibly a king, wearing his characteristic (red) cloak; Wadsworth Atheneum, Hartford, CT. Wadsworth Atheneum Museum of Art/ Art Resource, NY.

Figure 5.4. Bronze helmet of the "Corinthian" (all-over) type, of the period of the Battle of Plataea; British Museum. © The Trustees of the British Museum.

of what always seems to be peculiarly hot central Greece, the lighter the better, from one point of view. On the other hand, the sturdier the armor, the better the protection against a hail of Persian arrows, or the charge of a Median steed. In any case, the hilly and broken nature of the terrain would probably have rendered standard phalanx tactics—whatever they now standardly were (another point of scholarly dispute)—difficult if not impossible. Moreover, the scale and nature of the opposition and the unprecedented duration of the confrontation are good further arguments in favor of the employment of tactics that were more opportunistic than orthodox.

It was perhaps such narrowly military factors and considerations that partially account for the—to some observers unaccountable—delay of some eleven days in bringing matters to a head and then a conclusion. Within that timespan what may have been the most significant event—to call it a tipping-point is probably excessive—was the killing of the huge and unwieldy Persian cavalry commander Masistius. This was accomplished by a crack Athenian hoplite task force supported by archers (and was later made much of by the Athenians, see chapter 6). But the delay itself is not by any means inexplicable; political considerations and difficulties other than military ones must also be factored in. On the one hand, Pausanias could still have been hoping for yet more troops to arrive, so that he might feel there was safety in numbers if nothing else; on the other hand, he was totally inexperienced as a general, the size and composition of his allied army were in any case unprecedented, and general morale cannot have been exceptionally high, if indeed there was not a considerable mood of despair—a mood which would not have been relieved by a series of allegedly negative omens produced by seers (*manteis*) from the entrails of sacrificed animals.

What triggered the final evolutions was another, unfortunate consequence of the delay—an increasingly critical shortage of food and especially water, aggravated by Mardonius' cavalry's first capturing a Greek provisions convoy and then blocking a vital spring. Hence Pausanias' decision to order a retreat, which—a Spartan touch, this, since Spartans, as we have seen, were trained to maneuver in darkness—was to be accomplished at night. According to Herodotus' account, at all events, just about everything that could go wrong in such a complicated maneuver did go wrong, including an alleged incidence of gross—and very un-Spartan—insubordination by a regimental commander called Amompharetos. Many details of that story, however—including reference to voting with a pebble, which was an Athenian not a Spartan practice—look to me to have been fabricated by a non- or anti-Spartan source. If genuine, it would in any case have been a solitary exception to the rule of unquestioning Spartan obedience—and there are always exceptions to any rule.

But what if the retreat had been planned by Pausanias—as a lure to get Mardonius to abandon his cavalry harassment tactics (which had been proving all too successful) and commit himself to a direct engagement on the far, southern side of the Asopos? As a sort of land-based copy of the lure by Themistocles that had proved fatal to Xerxes at Salamis the previous summer? At any rate, Pausanias, who like Leonidas before him represented the allegedly senior of the two Spartan royal houses, the Agiad, would not have been the last Spartan royal commander to exploit deception in warfare; King Agesilaos II (reigned c. 400–360) from the other (Eurypontid) Spartan royal house would bear ample witness to that. Nor was he the last Spartan commander to rely on—or exploit—divine signs from sacrificial entrails in his favor, as we shall see. At all events, he won decisively the battle of the *manteis* no less than the actual hand-to-hand battle on the Plataean field. This may have been fought, finally, on the calendrical day that the Athenians knew as Boedromion 4, and the Boeotians as Panemos 27—the day, according to the much later (c. 100 CE) Boeotian litterateur Plutarch (*Life of Aristeides* ch. 19), "on which the Hellenic Synod still meets at Plataea, and the Plataeans sacrifice to Zeus the Liberator." That could equate to our September 19th, though that doesn't mean that the day of the final battle itself fell necessarily towards the end of the third week of September; at most we can say that it must have happened several weeks after the end of June, when Mardonius had occupied Athens.

Nor can the precise location or the exact evolution of the climactic battle be certainly recovered since, on top of the usual uncertainties in reconstructing any ancient battle (Whatley 1964), we do not know where "the island" that Herodotus mentions was located nor where the Persian cavalry were "separately" deployed. The alleged total noninvolvement of the Persian center, supposedly 40,000 men under Artabazus, is a further enigma. Moreover, to confuse matters further, the most conspicuous remains of ancient Plataea (at modern Kokla) lie further north, into the plain, than the probable site of the fifth-century BCE city. But certain things do seem clear. Pausanias and his Spartiates and other Laconians took on Mardonius and his elite Persian infantry, who had in the event unwisely launched the last assault and so commenced what the Greek novelist Nicholas Snow (Professor Nikolaos Kyriazis) nicely calls the "dance of death." But Pausanias responded only after what—to an outside observer at least—looks like playing politics with the usual and required pre-battle sacrifices. Claiming that the omens were not yet favorable, he allowed the Tegeans to respond to Mardonius first, while he prayed instead to the Plataeans' goddess Hera. Opportunely, the sacrifices yielded the correct positive result (see further below). On their left wing, the Athenians maneuvering to their right (eastwards) encountered and defeated the various "medizing" Greeks, including Thessalians and Boeotians, and especially— with a vengeance, no doubt—the Thebans.

The battle proved a lengthy one by ancient Greek standards, according to which they were usually over in a few hours at most, and it involved a great deal of "shoving" (*ôthismos*), which probably was quite a regular feature of most battles. After the initial shock of encounter between the opposing front ranks, if neither one instantly gave way—or ran away— there would be a pause for regrouping. A number of individual contests might break out at various points in the immediate killing zone, but on top of that there would have been the shoving done by the ranks behind those immediately engaged at the front, as hoplites leaned into their hollowed shields, placing them on the backs of the soldiers in front both to encourage them forward psychologically and to propel them forward physically. The Greeks' eventual victory was at any rate due to ordinary soldiers rather than to the genius of their commanders, and to their decisively superior arms, discipline and—when it came to the crunch—morale. However, Pausanias, young and inexperienced as he was, does also deserve a considerable share of the credit for sticking to a simple plan of counterattack and for somehow contriving to hold more or less together an unprecedentedly huge and variegated Greek force for such a long period of duress in the face of what must have seemed to many to be irresistible barbarian might.

An especially key moment, given what we think we know about the top-down nature of Persian and other oriental societies of the time and their practices of military command, was the death of Mardonius. He was somehow killed by a Spartan whose descendants dined out thereafter on their ancestor's feat—or rather hand, if we are indeed to credit the story that he brained the Persian commanding general with a stone. (But perhaps, it has been cannily suggested, this proud Spartan family and the Spartans collectively had an interest in robbing of the true credit for the deed one of the many thousands of light-armed Helots involved in the battle?) The Persian camp was breached, and many Persian defenders were slaughtered. Herodotus, with his usual weakness for large sums, believed that only 43,000 on the Persian side survived, implying a casualty figure of over 200,000. Actually, 10,000 killed out of an original force of some 100,000 may be a much sounder estimate. As for the Greeks' casualties, he believed that only (precisely) 91 Spartans, 52 Athenians, and 16 Tegeans had been killed, a total of 159 that was smaller both in the aggregate and as a percentage even than the (again, precisely) 192 Athenians who had died at Marathon eleven years before. This is in line with the historian's overall view of the battle's significance, which he saw as a thumping triumph of the (relatively) few over the (innumerably massive) many.

Despite preferring Salamis to Plataea as the decisive battle, and the Athenians over the Spartans as the loyalists most responsible for the Greeks' ultimate triumph (7.139), Herodotus did nevertheless concede that Plataea was "the most splendid victory of all those about which we have knowledge" (9.64), and that in this battle individual named Spartans and the Spartans collectively had been the best fighters. In the lapidary formulation of Oxford historian George Cawkwell, from the Persian Great King's viewpoint "It was at Plataea, not at Salamis, that the new satrapy was lost."

As a footnote, I mention here an intriguing oddity, one that tends to reinforce my thesis about the serious religious significance attributed to the battle and the victory by the ancient Greek victors themselves. The Spartans believed, of course, that their victory could not have been won without the aid of the gods—both the gods in general and various more specific deities and divinities. In that respect, they were normal Greeks. However, that is by no means the whole story, for the Spartans' piety and religiosity were exceptional, even among the religious Greeks. As Herodotus put it, in an understatement whose significance all his hearers and readers would have instantly grasped, they "esteemed the things of the gods above those of mere mortal men" (5.63, 9.7). Well, all Greeks conventionally did that, so Herodotus must have been drawing attention to the particularly intense and unwavering quality of the Spartans' religiosity, which went hand-in-hand with one of their supreme societal virtues, that of *peitharchia* or obedience to authority. The gods as it were stood for them at the pinnacle of a chain of command that reached right down to the humblest Spartan and his humblest actions in everyday life, off as well as on the battlefield or drill-ground. But even that does not quite capture the peculiarity of the Spartans' religious outlook and behavior as applied to the Battle of Plataea. For they were convinced that the victory had been won for them, not alone by Pausanias and his Spartan warriors aided by their gods, but to a significant degree by a noncombatant in the literal, physical sense.

That is, they attributed it significantly to the efforts of their principal *mantis* (soothsayer, seer, diviner), Teisamenus; it was presumably he who had delivered to Pausanias the good news of favorable sacrificial omens at just the right, critical moment. And yet Teisamenus, though by then a Spartan citizen, had been by origin a foreigner from the allied, northwest Peloponnesian city of Elis, and he had not therefore endured the special childhood training that was for native Spartans one of the prerequisites of attaining adult citizenship. He was not, strictly, "one of us." Indeed, according to Herodotus, the grant of citizenship to him (and simultaneously to a brother of his) was unprecedented in the long annals of Spartan history, and it had been made precisely so as to secure his irreplaceable services in divining the will of the gods who presided over the fortunes of war. That is surely credible, even though it is odd in a way that the Spartans, who set such immense store by divination, not least in times of war and battle, should have felt that there was no locally born and bred Spartan capable of doing the same job. But perhaps the fact that Teisamenus was from Elis, the city which hosted the Olympic Games every four years and managed the sanctuary of Olympian Zeus too when the games were not on, had something to do with it, as the Spartans were always especially interested in the Games and always especially keen to keep on good terms with Zeus of Mount Olympus, the most powerful single divinity in the entire Greek pantheon. The Battle of Plataea thus became the first of the five "victories" that Teisamenus would win for his new fellow-citizens. Revealingly, in the same sense, it was for the Spartans' habit of paying minute attention to the niceties of discerning the views of the gods and giving them their due that a later commentator, Xenophon of Athens who knew Sparta well from the inside, would hail them as "craftsmen of Ares."

Another striking post-Plataea oddity worthy of special mention—concerning the Plataean citizen Euchidas—will be told elsewhere, in the context of the competitive intercity commemoration that forms the essence of the next chapter. Here, though, we must first wrap up the military narrative of 479. The Battle of Plataea was decisive militarily; never again did a Persian king think to invade and conquer any part of mainland Greece by land. But it was not actually the very last battle of the "Graeco-Persian Wars." That, to rub Attic salt in Xerxes' wounds, was the amphibious land-sea engagement fought on and off the Asiatic coast by the loyalist Greek alliance, which was by then represented chiefly by the Athenians and led by Pericles's father Xanthippus, at Cape Mycale near the eastern end of the island of Samos. Patriotic Greek tradition indeed held that Mycale was fought and won on the very same day as Plataea. But though it's regularly referred to as a "battle," such little evidence as survives for how it was fought suggests that it was more a mopping-up operation than a full-scale, military-naval encounter. At all events, it finally extinguished such fight as the Persians—and particularly Xerxes—might still have been willing to put up at sea. The Persians had fought bravely on land, so Herodotus relates, but the Phoenician fleet was it seems still suffering from post-Salamis traumatic shock disorder.

Not that this was the last bellicose encounter of Greeks with Persians, by any means. Apart from the literal battles fought during the roughly "fifty-year period" (Pentecontaëtia) that elapsed between the Persian and Peloponnesian Wars and those of the fourth century, we have to consider the metaphorical battles for post–Persian Wars primacy of memorialization fought out between different Greek states on the winning as well as on the losing side. These will be the subject of the next chapter and, as we shall see, they involve, eventually but crucially, the Oath of Plataea.

6

THE GREEKS INVENT THE
PERSIAN WARS

The Mythology and Commemoration of Plataea

"The Hellenes" fought the war against the barbarian Persians— so ran the patriotic rhetoric and mythology. But in hard and nasty fact "the Hellenes" very quickly dissolved after the war was over into separate, antagonistic groups and groupuscules. Sparta and Spartans were quickest off the mark, not surprisingly, in an effort to enshrine in public Greek memory forever their role at Plataea, as having been the decisive role in the entire Graeco-Persian conflict. The Athenians, however, were equally quick to try to push the claims of Salamis over Plataea, a project with which they had some considerable success, not least because they already had Marathon as a victorious platform to launch themselves from. The considerable claims of the little city of Plataea itself for memorializing mention tended to get squeezed between the fists of the two much greater Greek powers, despite its being the site of religious commemorations that were ostensibly "Panhellenic" rather than either nationalistic or sectarian.

THE GREEK ART OF MEMORY

In their art of memory, as with so many other key cultural artifacts of theirs, the ancient Greeks were quintessentially agonistic, indeed antagonistic: competitive to the ultimate degree. Competition affected not just the matter of how great deeds were celebrated and commemorated but also the issue of which deeds, which battles, were to be celebrated, and by whom. Religious cult and ritual, sculpture, other kinds of monuments, and many different sorts of literary and epigraphical texts were laid under contribution in a seemingly never-ending war of absolutist values and relativist status-ranking. One neat way of bringing out the full force of these mutual comparisons and contrasts is to pit (with Jung 2006) the Athenians' celebration of Marathon against the Greeks' both collective and individual celebrations of Plataea. Unlike the memorial tradition of Marathon, which was overwhelmingly that of a single city (the Athenians conveniently suppressing as far as they possibly could any mention of their allies from—ironically—Plataea), the Plataea battle was commemorated both by a Panhellenic community collectively and, concurrently or rather competitively, by individual cities and citizens according to their individual traditions.

Put differently, though the Plataea victory was actually a Panhellenic accomplishment, almost immediately its memory or rather memorialization became a focal point of contention among eternally rivalrous Greeks and their cities. Space does not allow a full exploration of the highways and byways of this classically Greek cultural experience, but here follow some markers along various of the routes taken.

THE DEMOCRATIC ATHENIAN WAY

Following the democratic reforms introduced by Cleisthenes in 508/7, the Athenian citizen body was divided for civic purposes in both peace and war into ten cunningly artificial "tribes." Thus Athens' hoplite army fought in ten tribal regiments, each represented by its own popularly elected "general." Likewise, public funerary commemorations of Athenian hoplites who died in battle were organized by tribe, and only very recently indeed there came to light part of the communal monument to the dead "Marathon-fighters" of the tribe Erechtheïs—named after the legendary ancestor of the Athenians himself, the human but heroized Erechtheus. (He was celebrated and commemorated also in the name of the Erechtheum, the principal religious shrine of the city's divine patroness, Athena of the City, situated prominently on the south side of the Acropolis and distinguished externally by its famous Caryatid porch.)

Erected originally at Marathon itself, the tribal monument of Erechtheïs was transported some six and a half centuries later to the eastern Peloponnese, to the estate of a very distinguished and seriously rich Athenian, Herodes Atticus. Here is how the text begins (in the translation of Peter Thonemann):

ERECHTHEÏS
Fame, as it reaches the furthest limits of the sunlit
  earth,
Shall learn the valour of these men: how they died
In battle with the Medes, and how they garlanded
  Athens,
The few who undertook the war of many.

There then follows a list of names, twenty-two in all—just names, but no pack drill as it were, in the egalitarian, democratic Athenian way; in particular, no mention was made of their patronymics (father's names) because that might have been thought socially divisive, and Athens liked to maintain the glorious fiction that at least in death, especially if they had died fighting valiantly for their city, all Athenians were equal.

Likewise treating all dead citizens who died in war alike, and all alike as heroes, Athenian democratic oratory developed over the fifth century the genre known as the *Epitaphios Logos* or Funeral Speech, invented probably in the mid-460s. Absolutely standard and required, at least so far as the few extant real and fictitious examples of the genre attest, was a central and favorable mention of the Marathon victory and/or of the men of Marathon, the heroized Marathonomachae ("Marathon-fighters"). Here it is, for example, in the version of the *Epitaphios* Thucydides attributed to Pericles—delivered in winter 431/430:

> always they bury the war dead in the People's Cemetery, excepting that is the men who fell at Marathon: those, in a way adjudged befitting their supreme virtue, they granted a burial actually at the site of their deaths.

That public oration was just one of any number of religious-cum-political manifestations that the Athenians produced after the Graeco-Persian Wars. Others included the founding of commemorative religious festivals and the incorporation of imprecations against the Persians in the prayers with which they began every meeting of their Assembly. Besides those, a host of images, inscriptions, and dedications was deployed to laud their city's military achievements; civic, religious, dramatic, and sporting events affirmed their status as a warrior community; and they endlessly expressed their martial virtues in drama (comedy as well as tragedy), in philosophy, in history, and—not least—in formal oratory, especially the *Epitaphios*.

In 480, exactly a decade after Marathon, the ante had been upped considerably by the almost as glorious and principally Athenian naval victory at Salamis. 2,485 years after that, in 2006, on September 29th—the supposed actual day of the battle—an impressive bronze sculptural monument to

Salamis designed by the happily named Achilles Vasileiou was erected on the islet of Salamis itself. But the ancient Greeks, with the Athenians naturally to the fore, had long beaten their descendants to it. Not at Salamis but at Delphi, the navel of the universe, in Apollo's Panhellenic sanctuary "the Hellenes" had already erected a monument in that precise name (if the reading of the stone is correct). They thereby set very high the bar above which the Spartans would have to rise if they were to take their place as leaders of the Greeks in final victory over the Mede—as indeed they did, the following year. But first let us consider those most nearly affected and afflicted by the battle of Plataea.

PLATAEA TOWN

The small town of Plataea, ethnically Boeotian but aligned politically since 519 BCE with Athens across the Boeotian frontier, took responsibility for commemorating the many fallen Greeks. This was yet another assertion of independence from Thebes (which never forgave Plataea for its ethnic "treason") but also a tribute in particular to the ally, Athens, with whom it had fought shoulder-to-shoulder at Marathon, and bench-by-rowing bench at Salamis. To be distinguished from the Oath, and likewise controversially authentic, is the so-called Covenant of Plataea, ably discussed by among others Oxford historian Russell Meiggs (1972: 507–8). The source for it is Plutarch (about whom more anon) in the *Life* he composed in c. 100 CE of one of the greatest Athenian heroes of the Persian Wars period, Aristeides. According to this

(Plut. *Arist.* 21.1–2), Aristeides had immediately after the Plataea battle made a number of proposals to the still more or less united allies of the Hellenic League, namely:

1. There should be an annual political-religious meeting at Plataea.
2. There should be inaugurated an Eleutheria (Freedom) festival to be held every fourth year.
3. A common allied force should be raised to carry on the fight against the barbarians, consisting of 10,000 shields (presumably hoplite infantrymen), 1,000 horse, and 100 ships (some 20,000 sailors including officers and other supernumeraries).
4. The people of Plataea (whose town was currently still in a state of destruction) should be declared sacrosanct and, on behalf of all Greeks, conduct an annual sacrifice to the many fallen of Plataea.

There seems even less room for maintaining the authenticity of this "Covenant" than that of the Oath. There is thus no mention of it in other, more nearly contemporary extant sources where it would have been expected: for conspicuous instance, in the speech of "the Plataeans" in Book 3 of Thucydides' *History* of the Peloponnesian War, where in a context of 427 BCE the Plataeans are desperately pleading their cause before the Spartans against the Thebans. The upshot of that "debate" was that the Spartans took a line that was utterly disrespectful of the supposed "Covenant," by gratifying the Thebans in destroying the city of Plataea the following year.

PAUL CARTLEDGE

There is no evidence of annual meetings being held even in the fifth century BCE. No Freedom Festival is firmly attested before the mid-third century BCE (Strabo 9.2.31, 412; Paus. 9.2.6). Finally, the wrong sort of force (too few ships are specified, as against too many hoplites) is here envisaged for the kind of struggle that would have been considered necessary in 478 and was in fact shortly to be introduced under the Athenians' hegemony of their so-called Delian League, of which Aristeides was the moving spirit.

Without much doubt, some sort of all-Greek allied meeting is likely to have been held, possibly even at the holy site of Plataea, or at the even holier site of Delphi nearby, sometime soon after Plataea. One—not the least important—thing they will certainly have collectively decided on is the form and content of the allied Greek victory monument that was to be erected, suitably inscribed, at Delphi. Known for short as "the Serpent Column," this took the form of a coiled snake made of bronze issuing in three snake heads at the top, which together supported a golden tripod-cauldron (see further chapter 7). But whatever else the allies really decided, it will not have been to adopt this Covenant. Rather than to the facts of the 470s, this supposed document belongs, I suggest, to the process of later, indeed much later mythopoiesis, in this case not Athenian but Plataean. No doubt its existence was asserted if not faked by the Plataeans partly in order to aid religious tourism, as Meiggs himself suggested, but I believe that in its original form it may belong not all that far in time from the inscription of our Oath at Acharnae, and share a like inspiration. More specifically, I would link it to the third (after those of 480 and 426) destruction within the period of little over a century of the city of Plataea, this one inflicted in 373 by the Thebans, which provoked a justly anguished pamphlet from the stylus of the prolific and Panhellenist Athenian *rhetor* Isocrates. But, even if that were not enough to prompt the Covenant's original invention, then the sacking of Delphi by the Phocians in the 350s, including the sacrilegious melting down of the tripod-cauldron that had sat atop the Serpent Column since 478 or so, surely would have been.

Finally in this section I mention a curious anecdote involving Plataea and Delphi that supposedly refers to an event immediately after the Battle of Plataea. In fact, I shall suggest, it should be placed and interpreted within a much later, ideological context, involving commemorative competition between little Plataea and—at least formerly—mighty Athens. The anecdote is told by Plutarch, a Boeotian himself and also a priest at Delphi, in the same *Life* of Aristeides (ch. 20). As Plutarch records it, no doubt from personally having seen it, Euchidas's epitaph read—or at least included the sentence:"Euchidas having run to Delphi returned here on the very same day." The story local informants spun for the inquisitive Plutarch to account for this curious epitaph went like this. After the Battle of Plataea Euchidas had simply flown off on winged feet to sacred Pytho, that is to Delphi, the holiest seat of the great oracular god Apollo. This he did out of piety in order to fetch from the shrine's hearth a portion of sacred fire with which to purify Plataea from the pollution inflicted by the barbarian Persians on his home city—and perhaps from that inflicted on other Greek sites too. What caused his exceptionally informative sepulchral commemoration was not just his piety, however, but the—supposed—fact that he ran there and back, a distance that Plutarch puts at 1,000 stades (about 190 km or 114 miles), "on the very same day." More precisely, Euchidas allegedly returned from Delphi to Plataea before sunset "and then shortly after expired." Personally, I not only find that feat physically impossible but also believe that it belongs in a characteristic context of intercity competitive commemoration, the competitors in this case being Plataea and Athens. For if the Euchidas anecdote reminds you of the one about an Athenian (variously named) who allegedly ran from Marathon to the city of Athens, a distance of only some 40 kilometers, to report the great victory of 490 BCE, and then immediately expired after barely managing to gasp out his good news, you would not be greatly in error. Which city invented its anecdote first is impossible to say, but since the Euchidas story is the more fantastic of the two, perhaps the temporal if not necessarily the creative priority should be given to Athens.

THE SPARTAN WAY

Lacking the Athenians' taste and aptitude for formal public speechifying, the Spartans compensated in other verbal ways, above all as we shall see by commissioning works in poetic genres that they did find culturally acceptable and even congenial: the quintessentially laconic epigram, and contemporary versions of the age-old Homeric heroic epic. Elaborate public architecture had never been the Spartans' thing, either, yet—as we learn from a much later (first century BCE/CE) literary source, Vitruvius, writing under Roman emperor Augustus—the Spartans did erect, presumably some time in the 470s, a war-memorial known as the Persian Stoa (Colonnade). Stoas in the Greek world generally were attractive urban features providing shade and seating for passing the time of day more or less idly, or for staging formal civic procedures such as lawsuits, but in Sparta leisure was not at a premium and the civic center was barely urbanized. For instance, the name given to the space where the Spartans met in assembly was "Skias" or Sunshade, indicating a temporary awning rather than a marked architectural space such as the Pnyx at Athens. So the Persian Stoa was in itself a hugely exceptional oddity, which by the time of the traveler Pausanias (mid-second century CE) was, he reckoned, the most eye-catching sight of the Spartan Agora. However, there is good reason for supposing that the architectural elaboration—including the substitution for normal columnar pillars of images of bound Persians and reference to the Battle of Salamis—described by Vitruvius and Pausanias was the result of a makeover effected in the period of Roman Emperor Augustus, and not part of the original fifth-century BCE concept (Spawforth 2012: 118–21). The inclusion in the remodeling of a sort of caricature of the beautiful female Caryatid pillars of the Athenians' Erechtheum strikes a particularly incongruous note. The name "Caryatid" may conceivably have been derived from Caryae, a town of the Perioecic "out dwellers" on the northern border of Laconia, Sparta's city-territory, but it is highly unlikely that it would have been so had Caryae really, as Vitruvius reports, "medized"—favored the Persian side—in 480, unlike all other such Laconian towns.

It was typically outside Sparta, however, that the Spartans preferred to make their commemorative splashes, and particularly at the two major Panhellenic shrines. Thus, at some point in the second quarter of the fifth century they both added a golden shield to the pediment of the newly built Temple of Olympian Zeus at Olympia and dedicated in that same shrine a large bronze image of Zeus, with the accompanying message inscribed on its base:

Receive, O lord Cronos' son Olympian Zeus, [this] beautiful *agalma*
With propitious spirit, from the Lacedaemonians.

An *agalma* was literally a thing in which Zeus was expected to take delight; it was one of the regular Greek words for "statue." It rather takes the breath away, though, to think that what the Spartans may have been thanking him for in this instance was his aid in putting down yet another rebellion of their own domestic slave population of Greek Helots.

With some relief we turn to the victory monument of all victory monuments, the so-called Serpent Column set up at Delphi (see Fig. 6.1). As mentioned above, on a stone base was set an upright coil of bronze issuing in three snake heads upon which rested a gleaming gold cauldron. Across the coils there was inscribed in the local Delphian alphabet a very spare text listing at any rate most of the Greek loyalist allies, in groups of three and in some sort of order of priority. We can't say how tall the whole monument originally was because it does not survive intact. Some of the base has been excavated at Delphi, and perhaps part of one

Figure 6.1. The official monument dedicated by the victorious Greeks to Apollo at Delphi (subsequently removed to Constantinople/Istanbul, where its partial remains subsist in the old Hippodrome) took the form of a coiled, triple-headed snake, whence "Serpent Column"; above the snakes' heads originally was perched a golden cauldron. Vanni/Art Resource, NY.

of the snakes, but whatever else is extant was found and can mostly still be seen, not at Delphi but in today's Istanbul. That city was called originally Byzantium (Byzantion in Greek spelling), but its name had been changed to Constantinople by the very Roman emperor, Constantine I, who had the remaining monument transported there, to his Hippodrome, to enhance his new eponymous world capital. I say "remaining monument" because already in about 350 BCE the local Phocians, then engaged in a fierce war with King Philip II of Macedon for control of Delphi, had had the golden cauldron melted down to provide funds to pay (foreign but Greek) mercenaries. At all events, the Serpent Column would originally have been mightily impressive, and its striking appearance would have been enhanced by its precise location within the sanctuary in relation to the Temple of Apollo and to other, competing monuments (see further below).

The text on the coil began laconically: "These fought the war." The list of 31 names that follows also began laconically in another sense: it was headed by "Lacedaemonians" (Spartans). Immediately after them came "Athenians," but to the ancient Greek way of thinking that meant, symbolically, a long way after. There were no second prizes, no silver medals, at the ancient Olympic or Pythian Games.

OTHER PANHELLENIC OFFERINGS

The "spatial politics of Panhellenism" (Michael Scott's apt phrase) were nasty, brutish, and quite prolonged. Thus, the Serpent Column was very much not a stand-alone item at Delphi. Rather, it was directly and deliberately pitted *against* the monument erected by Sicilian Greek strongman Gelon, dictator of Syracuse, to commemorate his victory over the Carthaginians at Himera that was allegedly won on the very same day as Salamis. Gelon in his own peculiarly grandiloquent way was attempting a Panhellenic statement of sorts, linking the freedom from would-be barbarian conquerors achieved militarily by the Greeks of the (newer, colonial) West to that of the Greeks of the old Greek heartland. But his monument was excessively personal, too self-aggrandizing, insufficiently Hellenic, and in pretty flagrant contradiction of the Delphic maxim "nothing in excess." Both victory monuments were sited very prominently on the "prime real estate" of the eastern terrace of the major Apollo temple (which itself bore that maxim), but the Serpent Column was the more centrally positioned.

Zeus's shrine at Olympia too, for all that it attempted to express a noncompetitive and genuinely Panhellenic ideal, witnessed a battle royal of commemorations. It was here, in the Spartans' backyard as it were, rather than at Delphi, that the helmet Miltiades had worn at Marathon was piously dedicated, bearing the simple legend "Miltiades." The location of the dedication—not made where one might have expected it, on the Athenian acropolis—probably owed a lot to intense internal Athenian politics. Just one year after the heroics of Marathon, Miltiades was prosecuted by his rival Xanthippus (father of Pericles) for committing an impiety on the island of Paros, found guilty and fined a colossal sum—though he died before he could pay it. His son Cimon did eventually pay it off. But its presence at Olympia will not have been lost on the major Peloponnesian power, the Spartans, who had failed to turn up for Marathon in time and probably will not have been amused by the implicit reference. As for the battle of Plataea, that was commemorated by a communally dedicated statue of Zeus facing east near the entrance to the Bouleuterion (Council-chamber). Its base survives with an inscription, but so too does an oriental helmet with an inscribed official dedication by "the Athenians." Panhellenism was an ideal that was very rarely attained in lived practice. Just consider further the other two major Panhellenic shrines, Isthmia (in honor of Poseidon) and Nemea (another devoted to Zeus). They, together with Olympia and Delphi, had been locked for competitive athletic purposes into an eternally recurring, outwardly harmonious cycle of athletic festivals for almost a century, since the 570s. Yet although a commemorative statue of Zeus was set up for Plataea at the Isthmia sanctuary, as at Olympia, commemorations—let alone celebrations—of any kind were conspicuous only by their absence from Nemea. The explanation lies in Greek festival politics. Whereas Olympia was managed by a second-rate city, Elis, Nemea was in the hands of the ultra-ambitious and potentially much more powerful city of Argos—always Sparta's deadliest rival for Peloponnesian hegemony, and a city that de facto if not quite formally had taken the path of medism in 480–479.

REGENT PAUSANIAS

From Sparta's official commemorations we must distinguish the personal and excessive, indeed hubristic, self-promotion of the Greeks' overall commander-in-chief at Plataea, Regent

Pausanias. In the context of the battle's immediate aftermath Herodotus had drawn a sharp contrast between the simple, austerely self-denying, typically Spartan mores of Pausanias and those of the defeated Persians. But, as Edward Bulwer-Lytton sagely remarked in 1837, "It is often that we despise today what we find it difficult to resist tomorrow," and he may well be right that it was the vast booty heaped on Pausanias by grateful Greeks that "ruined in rewarding him." At all events, Pausanias committed the heinous faux pas of having a boastful, self-aggrandizing message added to the base of the Serpent Column to the effect that he himself, as "leader" of the Greeks, had somehow been solely responsible for their collective victory. A faux pas which he within a few years advanced unpardonably further by appearing to be more eager to join the Persians than he was any longer to beat them.

Adding injury to medizing insult, he was debited officially by the Spartans in authority with meditating a drastic extension of the jealously guarded Spartan citizen franchise to—horrors!—Helots specially liberated for that purpose. For this, almost the ultimate un-Spartan criminal activity, he was summoned home posthaste from Byzantium and incarcerated. He was imprisoned moreover within not secular but sacred space: in the principal shrine of the city's patron goddess, located on the Spartan acropolis, where she was worshipped under the alternative titles of "City-holding" (Poliachos) Athena and Athena "of the Bronze House" (Chalkioikos). The latter sobriquet was owed to the decoration of the temple's inner walls, adorned as they were with bronze plaques presumably bearing some kind of pictorial decoration. This was a relatively rare Spartan concession to nonutilitarian aesthetics, though in earlier times—and this temple decoration may date back to 550 BCE or earlier—the Spartans seem to have been markedly less "spartan" than they had famously become by the fifth century.

Here therefore the wretched Pausanias came perilously close to inflicting a general miasma of pollution on his fellow citizens by dying from starvation within a sanctified space. As it turned out, however, he was released within a whisper of his dying breath, and the Spartans themselves sought later to atone for their near-sacrilegious error by setting up two statues in his honor and—much later still—establishing a new annual festival to his memory, jointly with that of the unambiguously unsullied Persian War hero, Leonidas. In some mitigation of Pausanias' guilt, it has to be said that his already severely inflated ego will hardly have been cut down to size by the best efforts of our next commemorative witness, who hailed from the Aegean island of Ceos (modern Kea).

SIMONIDES

Pride of place and pole position in the Spartans' race for patriotic self-advertisement went to the leading poet-propagandist Simonides, who apart from his almost peerless praise-singing was famed in after times as a pioneer of mnemotechnics. Anne Carson, the brilliantly original poet-classicist of our own day, has acutely written, in a special study setting off Simonides against another, far more tragic poet-memorialist, Paul Celan (Carson 1999): "As a poet who wrote on stone, Simonides had reason to concern himself with the processes of excision, eliding and removal of surface. To carve an inscription on stone is to cut away everything that is not the meaning."

Simonides' two-line epigram on the Spartan dead of Thermopylae is the neatest possible illustration of those processes and has justly become world-famous:

Go, tell the Spartans, stranger passing by,
That here, obedient to their laws, we lie.

This constitutes also a memorably exaggerated version of the "beautiful death" motif that the Spartans had long made peculiarly their own, if in their typically idiosyncratic way. For the only male Spartans who were permitted the honor of a gravestone with their name incised upon it were those warriors who died "in war"—and those two words together with the dead warrior's name were the total permissible extent of the epitaph. Herodotus saw a list of such names of the "300" (in fact, only 299 had died) at Thermopylae itself, and many years, indeed centuries, later a pious traveler (Pausanias) recorded seeing the copy of the list preserved back home in Sparta.

Much less well-known is an ode Simonides wrote on the same subject. We owe our knowledge of this to the Greek general historian Diodorus of Sicily, writing a compendious *Library of History* four centuries later than Simonides, in the second half of the first century BCE. He reported (11.11.6) that both compilers of histories and poets praised the *andragathia* (manly virtue) of the men of the Persian Wars and then quoted the ode:

Of those who died at Thermopylae
Renowned is the fortune, noble the fate:
Their grave's an altar, their memorial our mourning,
                              their fate our praise.
Such a shroud neither decay
Nor all-conquering Time shall destroy.
This sepulchre of brave men has taken the high
Renown of Hellas for its fellow-occupant, as
     witness
Leonidas, Sparta's king who left behind a great
Adornment (*kosmon*) of valour, imperishable
     renown.

                              [trans. Peter Green, 2006,
                                   slightly modified]

"Their memorial our mourning" (line 3) recalls Jay Winter's excellent 1995 book on reactions to the First World War, *Sites of Memory, Sites of Mourning*. But the key word in the original here is *kosmos* (order, orderliness) in line 9, translated by metaphorical extension "adornment" but at root meaning literally "orderliness" or "order," a thoroughly Spartan sentiment. Indeed, Herodotus (1.65) had labeled the all-encompassing military-political system of Sparta that he ascribed to the founding lawgiver Lycurgus precisely as a *kosmos*. No less to the point, Simonides used the very same trope in another, much more recently discovered and much more ambitious poetic production, a heroic, Homeric-style elegy. This was also composed presumably on commission from the Spartans, though what catches the eye above all is the exceptional prominence it accords to Spartan Regent Pausanias.

Within the past twenty years, seven fragments of this long poem have been identified and published. They were written on a Roman-period papyrus found a century ago at what was the ancient southern Egyptian town of Oxyrhynchus (roughly "Sharp-nosed Fishville," named after a type of fish considered sacred by the native Egyptians; that was before the town was swollen by Mediterranean incomers under the successive Greek and Roman occupations). The longest known fragment of the poem, itself incompletely preserved, musters over 40 lines and begins with an invocation of the death of Achilles at Troy and a celebration of the role of Homer as poet in commemorating his fame. But within only a few more lines Simonides is referring to himself as collaborator of the Muse and to Pausanias son of Cleombrotus, overall commander-in-chief at Plataea, as "the best man," who led the Spartans to undying glory. Clearly, Simonides' objective is to elevate the mundane Spartans of 479 BCE to parity of esteem or at least of mention with the greatest Greek heroes of yore, and by implication to place the Graeco-Persian Wars, and specifically the battle of Plataea, alongside and on the same plane as the Trojan War, thereby—not incidentally—ranking himself with Homer. Necessarily, elevation of the Spartans collectively and of Pausanias individually could be achieved only at the cost of relatively diminishing the achievements of other loyalist Greeks.

Simonides opens, in startling contrast to Herodotus, by having the Spartans march out splendidly, not clandestinely at night, accompanied symbolically by—and perhaps bearing images of—Castor and Pollux (Spartan Helen's brothers) and Helen's husband King Menelaus. Helen of Troy, it must be remembered, was originally Helen of Sparta. Simonides goes on to mention quite specific places and persons, including the adopted Spartan seer Teisamenus, and to offer some poetic details of the actual fighting at Plataea that are contradicted by Herodotus'—later, prosaic, far more reliable—account. Divine apparatus in the Homeric manner is much more prominent here than in Herodotus, as befits Simonides' overall interpretation, according to which the battle was won crucially thanks to various gods' assistance on the Spartan side.

This was the sort of interpretation that would have been music to the pious Spartans' ears. The Trojan War references would also sort very well with Sparta's initial post–Persian Wars desire to exploit Plataea as part of their "Panhellenist" claim to active military leadership of a united Hellas—a claim that, for military as well as diplomatic reasons, they were compelled to abandon as early as 477. From a much later literary source, as noted above, we had known of the so-called Persian Stoa. Thanks to the "new Simonides," we now know too that, besides that, the Spartans were prepared to go for broke in commissioning a magnificent and grandiloquent—very unlaconic—elegy.

A question mark still remains, however, over where the elegy might have been first performed: was it in Sparta itself, or in a Panhellenic sanctuary such as Isthmia, or at the very navel of the world and site of the Serpent Column victory monument, Delphi?

Before leaving Simonides, it is necessary to correct two possibly false impressions that may have been conveyed above. First, Sparta was by no means his only employer. He is known to have composed at least 32 Persian Wars–related epigrams in all, for many other Greeks besides the Spartans, including: one to accompany the dedication of an altar to Zeus at Plataea, an epitaph for men fallen in battle at probably Plataea, an epigram or epigrams for a dedication at Delphi commemorating the end of Persian Wars, and, most pointedly and poignantly, one that hailed the Athenians' feat at Salamis as "the most brilliant achievement ever at sea by Greeks or barbarians." Herodotus might have approved. Second, Simonides was not a mere Spartan stooge or hero-worshipper of Pausanias. For we know that he was also not shy of admonishing Pausanias to remind himself that he was human, not superhuman, mortal, not divine. This admonition is presumably to be associated with other evidence of Pausanias's overweening presumption. Following his high-handed treatment of the allied Greeks at Byzantium in the early 470s and his alleged defection to the Persian side in the later 470s and early 460s, the Spartans first had erased Pausanias' boastfully self-aggrandizing inscription at Delphi (above) and then, having recalled him peremptorily to Sparta, they in effect starved him nearly to death sacrilegiously within the shrine of their patron city-goddess Athena. It was one of ancient Greek history's little ironies that Sparta and Athens, cities which were unlike or even opposed to each other in so many other ways, yet agreed in the matter of the identity of their divine protectress.

HERODOTUS

Anyone who chooses to retell the story of the Graeco-Persian Wars has, in the words of Robin Lane Fox (2006), "to come to terms with this genius and his narrative, second only to Homer in the literary legacy of the ancient world." Herodotus himself was fully conscious of his debt to Homer, and might not have objected to the Roman-period Greek literary critic who praised his style as "most Homeric." But he was also a child of his intellectually revolutionary, fifth-century times and so alert to the possibility of the (negative) opposition between "myth" and "history." Indeed, on the only two occasions on which he used the word "myth," both in book 2 (on Egypt), he used it negatively to mean a false tale. That cut no ice with Aristotle, who in his treatise on literary criticism (the *Poetics*) dismissed Herodotus precisely as a *muthologos*, a teller of (tall or mere) tales. This was not, however, an entirely objective judgment, since Aristotle considered all poetry, dramatic or otherwise, to be a superior intellectual activity to any form of history-writing. But ever since antiquity, there have been listeners and readers who share a version of Aristotle's view of Herodotus— as a fabulist, or myth-monger. I, while prepared to concede that Herodotus does present a somewhat mythologized Greek past or cultural tradition about the "Persian Wars," beginning with the Battle of Marathon in 490 BCE, am nevertheless quite a strong advocate of a (basically) truth-telling Herodotus.

His sort of myth-making was principally concerned, not to glorify the Athenians' or any other individual group of Greeks' self-image, but to point up, and to advocate, a practicable notion of genuine pan-Hellenic cultural solidarity. Composing as he was in the third quarter of the fifth century, when the Greek world was about to dissolve or was actually dissolving into the prolonged intra-ethnic *stasis* (civil strife) of the Atheno-Peloponnesian War (431–404 BCE), this advocacy seemed to him an imperative necessity. The cardinal passage to that effect is 8.144.2, taken with the earlier passage 8.3.1. In the former he placed in the mouth of "the Athenians," in a dramatic context of the winter of 480/79, a powerful statement of the overriding claims of "Hellenicity" (Hellenic identity). That was a notion which, they are made to say, was entirely proof against any attempt by bribery to make them turn traitor to the common Hellenic cause. In the earlier passage Herodotus had in his own voice roundly declared that "division within a kindred people (*stasis emphulios*) is as much worse than a united war against an external enemy as war is worse than peace" (8.3.1; quoted also in chapter 3). The latter part of that gnomic utterance echoes a sentiment already expressed very early on in his work through the proverbial dictum that in war fathers bury sons, whereas in peacetime, in accordance with the natural order of things, sons bury their fathers (1.87). This conscientious proto-pacifism was a very different project indeed from the sort of "nationalistic" or jingoistic myth-making—whether setting Greek *vs.* Barbarian or one Greek *polis* against another—in reference to the Persian Wars that, as we saw above, started up almost as soon as they were over.

It was only after 479 that Greek and especially Athenian literature and iconography fully developed the notion of the barbarian as "other"—ineradicably and unalterably different and inferior (Cartledge 2002). Herodotus would have no truck with that. Persians too could in his book be brave, for example, brave in the same way and to the same degree as Greeks. As for the often vicious Greek-Greek rivalry, including psychological-symbolical warfare over memorialization of the Persian Wars, Herodotus was again strikingly evenhanded—unlike, very often, his own hosts and auditors. Thus, after his account of Thermopylae but before he has come to write up Salamis, he proleptically awards the palm to the Athenians, as "saviours," for having made the most decisive contribution overall to the Greeks' ultimate victory in 480–479 (7.139). The stress on glory and memory remains paramount. But he is careful to preface that achingly controversial—as he too well knew—judgment with a telling disclaimer that reflected Athens' growing unpopularity: though he knew it would be unpopular with many, nonetheless he felt constrained to utter it since it seemed to him to be true. The approach or onset of the Peloponnesian War (see next subsection) would have made that judgment still more subject to reproach. Moreover, as we saw (chapter 5), Herodotus made a fairly good fist of providing an account of the battle of Plataea that, whatever else it obscured, did not hide the key and decisive role played in the Greek victory by Pausanias and his Spartans.

THUCYDIDES

The struggle over the memory of Plataea was intensified greatly by the outbreak and course of the Atheno-Peloponnesian War (431–404), the special subject of Thucydides son of Olorus of the Athenian deme Halimous. Thucydides consciously began his narrative chronologically where Herodotus of Halicarnassus (and later Thouria in south Italy) had left his off, in 478 BCE. But in no other sense, either official or informal, was he Herodotus' successor. There was as yet no branch of knowledge separately designated as "History," anywhere in the Greek world—or indeed elsewhere in the entire world at that date. And it is very noticeable, for example, that Thucydides surely deliberately avoided the very word by which Herodotus had laid claim to inaugurating a special branch of intellectual activity, namely *historia* in its original sense of "research or enquiry." Thucydides conducted such research, no question; indeed, unlike Herodotus, he makes a prefatory song and dance about the originality and superiority of his method of establishing what exactly happened in the significant human past (1.22). But perhaps one of his most important claims to historiographical fame is that he drew a sharp distinction between what people—individuals, groups (especially political factions) or states—publicly uttered or claimed as the reasons or motives for their actions and what really, truly, in Thucydides' own often sceptical and disabused view, those motives and reasons actually were (1.23). Thus he represents the ideological opposition between the two protagonists in his War as a case of Sparta posing as the would-be "liberator of Hellas" from the domination of an Athens imagined as a tyrant city. The behavior of both sides in the nearly thirty years' War, and the practical reactions of other cities and powers, would either corroborate, or more often give the lie to, such ideological claims of the protagonists. Emphasizing, like Herodotus, the theme of *stasis*, which he says (3.82) broke out more and more widely in the Greek world as the War progressed—or regressed, he both analyzes particular instances of *stasis* within individual Greek cities, and treats the War as a whole as one gigantic intra-Hellenic *stasis*.

The War actually broke out over—and physically at— Plataea, in the spring of 431, when Sparta's then ally, Thebes, attacked Athens' longstanding ally, Plataea, in peacetime. Two years later, in the summer of 429, the Spartans began a siege of Plataea. In Thucydides' narrative of the siege there is mention of an oath regarding Plataea that had been sworn in 479; but this turns out to refer not to any alleged pre-battle oath but to an oath allegedly sworn *after* the battle—an oath not to violate Plataea's autonomy. Which is precisely what the Spartans were then doing. After an eventually successful two-year siege, and a mock-trial of the Plataean survivors, the Spartans in 426 again ignored or rather trampled violently all over any such notionally pledged autonomy-oath, when they wiped Plataea off the map, literally. They were unforgiving of the Plataeans, in Thucydides' severely pragmatic view, because they were treating the dispute between the Thebans and the Plataeans in a purely utilitarian way, considering that the Thebans could be useful to them in the ongoing war with Athens.

The Athenians in reply attempted, with considerable justice, to cast Sparta as a traitor to the cause of the Hellenic unity that had been exemplified by the joint and common accomplishment at Plataea. They even went to the extreme lengths of granting collectively a new kind of Athenian citizenship specifically to those refugee Plataeans who took up residence in exile at Athens. To put that in context, Plataea had been allied with Athens since 519. Plataea and Plataea alone of Greek cities had sent a force to fight alongside the Athenians at Marathon in 490. Over and above the general Hellenic alliance of 481, therefore, the Athenians and the Plataeans enjoyed a special relationship. In 427 the Athenians not only gave these allied refugees physical asylum and symbolic support but created a new category of (not quite equal and full) citizenship specifically for these Plataean incomers. Since a Greek city's citizenship was always its most jealously prized and preserved political prerogative, by definition it was normally something acquired by birth and upbringing rather than by grant to an outsider or outsiders. Here and there, there were always exceptions—even xenophobic Sparta, as we saw, made two such *viritim* grants at precisely the climactic moment of the battle of Plataea. But for Athens to make a block grant such as this to citizens of another city, even if one that was long allied, was something really quite remarkable, as was acknowledged by the need to give it a special-category status and its own special "Plataean" designation. (In 405 the Athenians did go one step further and made a block grant of their citizenship to their loyal—and democratic—allies of Samos. This was a move of desperation, however, as Athens was on the brink of losing the Peloponnesian War, and was never repeated.)

Indeed, the Athenians went further even than that. Desperate to find some specifically Athenian contribution to the mainly Spartan victory at Plataea in 479, they fastened on the killing by Athenians of the giant Persian cavalry commander Masistius described in chapter 5. So important, retrospectively, did they consider this to have been that they commemorated it as conspicuously as they possibly could. They included what is surely intended as a depiction of it or allusion to it in a narrative relief frieze of the exquisite new Pentelic marble temple, which—through the usual democratic channels of Council and Assembly—they dedicated to Athena Nike (Victory) in the 420s (probably between 427 and 424) and arranged to have constructed at the very monumental gateway to the Acropolis. This lovely building and its handsomely carved decorative sculpture thus coincided, not at all coincidentally, with the Spartans' exiling of those pro-Athenian Plataeans whom they had not managed to kill in 427 and their brutal physical destruction of Plataea "foundations and all" (in the pointed formulation of Thucydides) in 426. (See Fig. 6.2.)

Figure 6.2. The Athenians' Temple of Athena Nike (Victory), c. 415/405 BCE, bore a relief frieze depicting a heroic victory of Athenians over Persians. © The Trustees of the British Museum.

It has further been suggested that there was a connection between this new Athena Nike temple and the process whereby Athens' ephebes, the young proto-citizens on the threshold of civic manhood, were formally inducted into the adult Athenian citizen community (see above chapter 3). At all events, this major Athenian monument is entirely relevant to the present book's overarching theme of ideologically motivated pseudo-historical commemoration. As is often the case, what may or may not actually have happened in 479 is one thing, what was made of the alleged event(s) later, by interested parties in different contexts and for differing purposes, is quite another.

CTESIAS AND EPHORUS-DIODORUS

A very different "historical" take on the Battle of Plataea, and indeed on the Persian Wars as a whole, may be gleaned from the surviving work of Ctesias of Cnidos (in southwest Asia Minor). Ctesias, a Greek subject of Persia, served as royal physician to Great King Artaxerxes II and indeed served him in that function at the battle of Cunaxa near Babylon in 401, where the reigning monarch defeated his full brother Cyrus, the young pretender. Xenophon of Athens fought as a mercenary on the opposite side; we can read his self-justificatory version in the *Anabasis*. Ctesias' *Persika* or "Persian History" had a much wider chronological scope than Xenophon's work, but is even less reliable. Perhaps it will be a sufficient commentary on its veracity and credibility as a record of the Persian Wars to point out that Ctesias appears—against all developmental logic and military sense—to have reversed the order of the battles of Salamis and Plataea. He also has Mardonius merely wounded rather than killed at Plataea, which reflects more what he thought his hellenophone Persian paymasters would like to hear than actual fact. In short, Ctesias' memoirs were those of a would-be "official" historian, and thus highlight by contrast what both Herodotus and Thucydides had aimed at in their respective works—unerring truth and unshakeable certainty, regardless of ideological slant.

About half a century after Ctesias, Ephorus—like him an Asiatic Greek, hailing from Cyme in Ionia—compiled a vastly larger history, indeed arguably the first Greek work of "universal" history in the sense that it purported to be an account of all Greek history down to his own day from the time of the at least semi-mythical post–Trojan War "Return of the Descendants of Heracles" to the Peloponnese; that would have been some time in what we would call the eleventh century BCE. Ephorus may have been a pupil at Isocrates' rhetoric school in Athens. At any rate, he wrote his thirty-book history at precisely the moment when the real contemporary Athens was busy inventing for itself a suitably imposing and patriotically heroic past in the third quarter of the fourth century BCE. Unfortunately, his work does not survive as such, but only in what are politely called "fragments" of possibly accurate later quotation. Most relevantly for us, however, as regards the commemoration of the Battle of Plataea, this is the work that stands in the shadows behind the oddly named *Library of History* compiled in the first century BCE by Diodorus, a Sicilian Greek. By and large, Diodorus preferred to operate with one main literary "source" for each period or region, and he seems to have used Ephorus as the source for his annalistic history of Greece in the fifth and fourth centuries. It was presumably therefore from Ephorus that Diodorus (12.29) took over his account and version of the Plataea oath, which is at least strongly reminiscent verbally of the Acharnae epigraphic text. However, both Diodorus' location of it and his timing of it, at the Isthmus of Corinth in 480 BCE, have no counterpart in Herodotus—one of several major differences of fact or emphasis between these two. Yet perhaps the single most telling discrepancy—a "give-away" indeed, betraying, I believe, the prejudices of Diodorus the Sicilian Greek rather than those of Ephorus the Asiatic Greek—is when Diodorus adjudges the victory won by Gelon, Greek tyrant of Syracuse, over the invading Carthaginians at Himera in northwest Sicily in 480 to be the "fairest" victory of all: not Herodotus' Salamis, let alone Herodotus' Plataea.

ATHENS AGAIN: THE FUNERAL SPEECH GENRE

As the power of Athens diminished to vanishing point, however, especially around the turn of the fifth to fourth century BCE, and again under pressure from the new kid on the block, Macedon, in the third quarter of the fourth century, so the Athenians' recollections of their ancestors' heroic deeds became more and more strident, and more and more "recovered" rather than authentic memories. There was no more strident or self-justifying native Athenian genre than that of the *Epitaphios* (Funeral Speech). This was a public, democratic institution invented perhaps in the 460s, as we have seen, and graced by at least two of Athens' greatest democratic orators, Pericles and Demosthenes. Plato in his *Menexenos*—a Funeral Speech supposedly delivered by Pericles but allegedly composed by his controversial partner in life, Aspasia of Miletus—rather foolhardily perhaps ventured a parody of the genre. But it was Demosthenes who in another kind of speech, a rabble-rousing oration delivered in 341 BCE before the Athenian Assembly (the *Third Philippic*), struck the authentically patriotic note: "there was something in the mentality of the people in those days, something we have now lost, which overcame the wealth of Persia and led Greece in freedom and was never conquered on land or sea." An earlier member of the canonical ten Attic orators, Lysias, originally from Syracuse but for long a democratically minded resident alien at Athens, had gone one better—almost inevitably in reference to Marathon: on that battlefield, he claimed hyperbolically, the Athenians and the Plataeans (mentioned for once! but Lysias was not Athenian-born) "secured a permanence of freedom for Europe."

It is precisely from this quasi-nationalistic strand of Athenian self-justifying, self-magnifying mythopoiesis, prevalent since at least the *Panegyric Oration* of Isocrates of c. 380, that in my view the Plataea Oath as preserved on the Acharnae stele somehow emerged. Soon after its inscription thereon (as noted in chapter 2), it was referred to in a forensic speech by the Athenian statesman-patriot Lycurgus (1.81). Lycurgus has a claim to be dubbed the Second Founder of democratic Athens, after the original founder Cleisthenes. But whereas Cleisthenes' democracy lasted, with interruptions and modifications, for over a century and a half (from 508/7), Lycurgus' Athens lasted less than fifteen years (336–322). Athens' major defeat at the Battle of Chaeronea in 338, at the hands of King Philip of Macedon and his son Alexander, necessitated major structural and ideological changes. The democracy itself was not suppressed by Philip, but it had to become a more "managed" democracy, and the management of it was entrusted to the aristocrat—and technocrat—Lycurgus to a degree that would have been considered unacceptable in the time of Pericles a century earlier. Lycurgus rather than Pericles far more nearly approximated to the status of "uncrowned king of Athens," as he took charge of Athens' finances and devoted himself to restoring and increasing both Athens' internal and external revenues. The surplus thereby achieved he was able to lavish on numerous public building projects, including a refurbishment of the Panathenaic stadium, a remodeling of the Pnyx area where the Assembly met, and a transmogrification of the seating in the Theater of Dionysus from mere earth and wood into permanent marble.

Soon after acceding to a position of what can properly be called power, Lycurgus began a public prosecution of a rival Athenian named Leocrates, whom he accused of desertion and dereliction of duty at the Battle of Chaeronea. The case did not actually come to court until 330, some half-dozen years later, at a time when Athens' powerlessness vis-à-vis a kingdom of Macedon now ruled by Alexander was all too patent and painful. What was required was a magnificent and magniloquent appeal to the Athenians' ancient patriotism, and this Lycurgus duly delivered, winning his case hands down. Whatever exactly Lycurgus actually said in court on that day, what we have to go by is the polished literary version he chose to "publish" subsequently. In this (1.81), the Oath of Plataea, Athenian-style, finds its perfectly appropriate place—just the sort of document to cause Athenian breasts to swell with nostalgic pride. It was no coincidence that Lycurgus was also intimately involved in promoting a new institution of the Athenian democracy that was intended somehow to remedy for the future the current tactical and ideological weakness of the Athenian military. That institution was the *ephebeia* or, anglicized, the ephebate, under the terms of which Athenians who were eighteen and nineteen years old were organized into a compulsory form of national service prior to being enrolled in the adult citizen army. Ephebes were nothing new, the ephebate was. Ready to hand as a kind of initiation-ritual formula for the new ephebes of the official ephebate was the Ephebes' Oath, a version of which had been handily inscribed on our stele at Acharnae immediately before our Oath of Plataea (chapter 3).

ANCIENT AFTERLIFE

Some time in the first century BCE, roughly contemporary with Diodorus of Sicily, Greeks from the eastern end of the Mediterranean fulsomely celebrated a revered ancestor. A long inscribed text, set up in a sanctuary of birth and marriage dedicated to Aphrodite in the territory of Salmacis, proudly proclaimed that "the land of holy Salmacis . . . brought forth Herodotus, the prose Homer in the realm of history. . . ." Not everyone, however, in the post-Classical Hellenistic and

Roman periods of Greek history viewed Herodotus as favorably as did his fellow Halicarnassians by any means. Notably, or notoriously, one ornament of the Greek literary movement sometimes labeled the "Second Sophistic" very firmly did not. This was the biographer, philosopher, and essayist Plutarch, who hailed from Chaeronea in Boeotia, not all that far from Plataea, and lived from c. CE 46 to 120.

Although it was one of the essential leitmotifs of the Second Sophistic movement (first century BCE to third century CE) to celebrate and recuperate the glories of classical Hellas, Plutarch in the years around 100 CE wrote a largely—not entirely—excoriating attack upon what he alleged to be the "mean-spiritedness" or "malignity" of Herodotus (its title in Latin is *De malignitate Herodoti*). Not the least of his complaints was directed against the monstrously biased (as Plutarch saw it) attitude adopted by Herodotus both to the "barbarian" Persian aggressors (palpably too favorable) and to the various Greek combatants. This was not, alas, Plutarch's finest intellectual hour. In hurling the derogatory epithet *philobarbaros* at Herodotus he came close to calling him the ancient Greek equivalent of a "wog-lover." As regards Herodotus' treatment of the various Greek cities and peoples involved, he was in Plutarch's warped view wildly too favorable to the Athenians, and grossly unjust to the Thebans. Plutarch was not himself from Thebes, but coming as he did from the relatively humble town of Chaeronea (the site of a number of major battles, including that of 338 BCE) he was a member of the ethnic grouping that called itself "the Boeotians." And he took up the intellectual cudgels on behalf of his fellow Boeotians of Thebes.

Plutarch could be favorable as well as hostile to Herodotus, though Christopher Pelling (2007) sees the spectrum of different attitudes represented in his voluminous oeuvre as due to the malleability of the several different genres of literature within which he worked. This view is borne out by John Marincola (2010, esp. 129–32), who has examined specifically the account of the battle of Plataea contained in Plutarch's already mentioned *Life* of Aristeides. Here, the biographer can be found both diverging from Herodotus' version (in relation to the pre-battle quarrel between Athens and Tegea) and following Herodotus (in respect of the heroic role he had accorded in the final battle to the Spartans). Where Plutarch shows himself most keen to distance himself from Herodotus, however, here as in the *De malignitate Herodoti*, is over the part played by the Thebans. For fellow-Boeotian Plutarch, the Thebans were collectively on the Persian side solely because their most influential citizens had medized eagerly, and dragged the ordinary majority of citizens along only unwillingly in their wake (18.7). Plutarch was a keen reader of Thucydides, and this was a line of argument, or of special pleading, already attributed to "the Thebans" by Thucydides, when giving his account of how Theban spokesmen in 427 BCE pleaded their savagely anti-Plataean cause before a tribunal of unforgiving and hardly impartial Spartan judges.

PAUSANIAS OF MAGNESIA

A year or so later, the Spartans did not scruple to destroy the city and expel its remaining pro-Athenian population, as already noted. So much for Plataea's status as a Panhellenic shrine of immortal honor. Although little Plataea did, after many further reverses, recuperate some reputation later, it was not until Greece itself had lost all meaningful political independence, to its Roman overlord and master, that the town was once again allowed to hold its head up high. The reign of Rome's first emperor, Augustus (27 BCE–14 CE) was a prime moment for the recovery of Plataea's prestige as an exemplar of how to confront and successfully resist barbarians, thereby ensuring freedom for oneself. Among other cultural manifestations Augustus, to mark his "victory" over the Iranian Parthians in 21 BCE, set up in both Rome and Athens respectively "a pair of massive tripods supported by kneeling barbarians in colored marble" (Spawforth 2012: 131). Simultaneously, the long-established Eleutheria (freedom) festival at Plataea acquired an enhanced aura, the renewed relevance of success in the race in armor (*hoplitodromos*) being attested at both Sparta and Athens, as well as hinted at at Didyma in Asia Minor. In short, there was something of a "renaissance" in the ceremonies at Plataea, officially endorsed by the emperor himself.

The principal extant literary witness to this archaeologically enhanced but spiritually and culturally debased (as he saw it) Roman Greece is the wistful and nostalgic religious itinerary compiled in the third quarter of the second century CE by one Pausanias, a Greek from Magnesia in Asia Minor and author of a *Periegesis* or travel guide. For Pausanias, the contemporary town of Plataea mattered far less than what it stood for as a monument of patriotic memory. He celebrated the victory of 479 BCE, he lovingly described at length the thank-offering statue of Zeus erected at the oldest Panhellenic shrine of Olympia that named the contributing cities in a similar way to the Serpent Column at Delphi; at Plataea itself he hailed the graves of the men who fought against the Persians; but not least of all he trumpeted, as mentioned, the fact that "to this day they still hold a contest in every fifth year that is called the Freedom games. . . . " This was a freedom whose meaning and symbolism had not lost all of its salience, but which had, alas, been voided of almost all of its practical content.

CONSTANTINE

It was no surprise, then, that the first avowedly Christian Roman emperor, the new Augustus, Constantine I the Great, when he transformed the old city of Byzantion into his own eponymous capital city of Constantinople, should have decided he needed the Serpent Column to adorn the new Rome of the East. And not only to adorn it but also to sanctify the city's links with the old Hellenic world, to enable it to draw on the old symbolic associations of Greekness that still had a major pull even as the Roman world under him rapidly Christianized. He therefore had the Serpent Column relocated to that city's ancient Hippodrome (horse racecourse), where it— or what is left of it—may still be viewed (Fig. 6.1).

7

CONCLUSION

The Legacy of Plataea

I n this book we have examined a number of central themes: the battle of Plataea itself, and its wider significance in its own and later ancient times; the significance of the inscribed Oath of Plataea as a historical source; and the impossibility of knowing with any certainty what took place in 479, or of judging with finality the authenticity of the Oath (inscribed and otherwise). But we historians, as I have tried to argue and show, are still able to make small but important gains even with only precious few—and a few precious—sources.

The book's themes have any number of contemporary resonances: culture wars over the politics of the past (compare the demand for reparations for slavery); multiple examples of "recovered" pasts (the modern Olympic Games movement);

modern war memorials, especially controversial ones, such as the holocaust memorial in Berlin or the Vietnam War Wall in Washington, D.C.; the study of the Oath (and its literary versions) as a sort of detective story; the battle of Plataea itself as a case study in ever-popular military history; or as an example of an unjustly forgotten—or at least often neglected and overlooked—battle (compare Leyte Gulf, possibly the largest naval battle in all recorded history, but . . .); the current debate over the virtues (or otherwise) of national military service; and, far from least, the role of religion in politics. Here, finally, I want to widen the angle and lengthen the depth of our vision by concentrating on just the first and the last of those "resonances."

For, looked at within a much longer timeline and broader conceptual frame, the Graeco-Persian Wars may also usefully be seen as The First World War of West *vs.* East. Indeed, arguably (in both senses), it was in the crucible of that decisive military conflict that a concept of "the West," devised as a polar opposite of "the East," was first forged. This is a thought that has been explored very carefully recently, both in more popular historical writings (Holland 2005) and in the more severely academic literature (Bridges et al. eds. 2007), and it has been taken up too by historians whose purview is more "global" or at least even more broadly "Western" (Pagden 2008). The underlying and sometimes explicitly expressed thought seems to be that, if the Greeks (some of them . . .) had not against all odds defeated the Persians, Western culture might today be somehow middle eastern (Iraqi, Persian, Assyrian, Babylonian . . .), rather than European or Euro-American, that is to say, ultimately, Greek or at any rate Graeco-Roman.

There is, however, room for contrary views, very contrary in the case of the late Edward Said, who saw in Aeschylus' tragic drama *Persians* of 472 BCE not just one of the earliest exhibits of Persian Wars literature but the very first exemplar of what he derogatorily labeled "orientalism" (1978, repr. 1995). By that he meant, far from the more or less innocent and scholarly study of matters eastern from a "Western" viewpoint, something akin to a criminal conspiracy to derogate, to put down, all facets of eastern cultures. No less provocatively, but no more persuasively to my mind, Arshin Adib-Moghaddam, a teacher of political science at the School of Oriental and African Studies in the University of London, has more recently (2008) sought to pour buckets of cold water on the whole East *vs.* West "clash of civilizations/cultures" notion, dismissing it as a fanciful construct that obscures of set purpose what—among other people and things—Europeans and Muslims, Americans and Arabs, and the Occident and the Orient share in common. But though he treats briefly of the Greek *vs.* Persian clash, his main focus and inspiration are much more modern, if not contemporary, political, cultural, and religious (especially Islamic) imperatives.

In the present book the main focal point of interest regarding the Persian Wars' reception throughout has been the specific conditions of the third quarter of the fourth century BCE, when the surviving Plataea Oath document was inscribed and put on display at Acharnae in Attica north of Athens. But as is amply demonstrated in the excellent Bridges et al. 2007 collective volume mentioned above, the Wars have in fact remained a source of provocation of cultural responses from

Antiquity to the present day. That volume begins with an essay on their historical impact on classical, that is fifth to fourth century BCE, Greece and ends with a discussion of Honorary Spartan Citizen Steven Pressfield's gripping and well-received Thermopylae novel, *Gates of Fire* (1998). In between, among the other very varied topics addressed are the events' impact on or reception by Plato, Plutarch, Byron, and George Grote, and their manipulation by painters, composers, playwrights, travelers, and filmmakers in scenarios ranging from the Ottoman world to Hollywood. Had the volume been put together a little later, it would no doubt have found room to discuss Frank Miller's strip-comic—as well as sometimes comical—treatment of Thermopylae that in 2006 became the basis of the ravingly, hair-raisingly successful movie *300*.

To which I now add a quite remarkable coda: not another filmic treatment or novelization, but nothing less than a secular scripturalization of the Graeco-Persian Wars. Into his *The Good Book: A Secular Bible* (2011), professional philosopher and atheist Anthony Grayling, founder of the New College of the Humanities, inserts what he calls a "book" with the ringingly Herodotean title, "Histories." The East/West distinction and opposition that appear elsewhere in this remarkable pseudo- or para-biblical confection are here given full rein: "the free hearts of the fathers of the West, smaller in number, weaker in power, yet stronger in resolve and greater in genius, kept the infant civilization free." Unfortunately, however, this seems to me to perpetrate what philosophers call a category error: for "the West" is not a properly historical construct. Moreover, I submit that, as is (too?) often the case with all cultural "receptions," this one says a good deal more about the state of the world in CE 2011, with its intensely renewed wars of religion on both the intellectual and the all too savagely practical planes, than it does about 479, or 350, Before the Common Era.

All the same, Professor Grayling does stand in an honorable tradition, which is indeed an unimpeachably ancient Greek one. As one of its founding fathers (Socrates) put it, or at least as he is said by his disciple Plato to have put it, "the unexamined life is not worth living for a human being." That clarion call is included in Plato's *Apology*, his version of Socrates' defense speech (in Greek *apologia*) at his trial in 399 BCE for improper religious observance (not duly worshipping the gods recognized by the city of Athens, and inventing new, unrecognized divinities of his own) and corrupting the young through his (anti-democratic as well as possibly impious) teachings. It failed to sway the 501 democratically selected jurors, who found Socrates guilty as charged—correctly, according to their own democratic lights (as I have argued in Cartledge 2009)—and condemned him, much more questionably, to death. There can be few aspects of life more worthy of our constant critical reexamination than our debt to our Hellenic cultural ancestors—as we, following the lead of the Romans and many others over the intervening centuries, have chosen to position and see them.

If I may therefore be permitted one concluding reflection of my own, as anachronistic no doubt as Plutarch's condemnation of Herodotus for mean-spiritedness, it would be this. Karl Marx, a classicist before he was a marxist, in a series of "theses" on the thought of Ludwig Feuerbach (1845) once famously declared: "The philosophers have merely interpreted the world, in various ways. The point, however, is to change it." Here is my paraphrase: "The historians have merely interpreted the Battle of Plataea and the Graeco-Persian Wars in general, in various ways. The point, however, is to end it—not discussion of Plataea and its reception, including the more or less wholly invented Oath, but . . . war, all wars, for ever." Or at any rate all unjust ones (cf. Walzer 2006, esp. 296–303, "Democratic responsibilities"; Fisher 2011).

Further Reading

I. Primary Sources

THE MAIN OATH TEXT

The stone with the inscription from the village of Menidhi (now officially re-named Acharnae) was uncovered in 1932 by a local farmer and bought from its finder through the good offices of Louis Robert, a famed French epigraphist (that is, specialist in reading and interpreting texts and documents inscribed on stone or bronze above all). This explains why it's now in the French School of Athens (catalogued as inv. no. I 7), and why it was he who delivered the *editio princeps* (1938: 296–316). Much of the most important earlier bibliography, including that work of Robert, is conveniently cited in Tod 1948: no. 204. More recently, see Rhodes & Osborne 2003: no. 88; Krentz 2007 (see further immediately below); and Kellogg 2008 (text and translation at 373–75; a very useful overview and review, but interested more in the Ephebic Oath than in the Oath of Plataea; cf. Kellogg 2005). I single out on the linguistic side a note by D. W. Prakken, who interestingly and provocatively calls the Oath "apoc-ryphal" and further suggests that "In all probability the language and system of orthography employed by this country priest [Dion] might have differed somewhat from the language of official decrees and the careful work of an official engraver under supervision" (1940: 64).

For an illustration of the stele's representation of a hoplite panoply in its "pediment," see Frontisi & Lissarrague 1998. On the style of the relief as a dating aid—not decisive—see Lawton 1995: 155. Sebillotte Cuchet 2007 is another detailed and illuminating discussion of the other "oath" text on the Acharnae stele, the Oath of the Ephebes; see also chapter 10 of her 2006 Paris thesis; and Siewert 1977 (see also next sub-section).

The most recent publication known to me is Platonos-Yiota 2004: 89–90, with a photo on p. 72; the volume as a whole (a "historical and topographical investigation of ancient Acharnae, the neighboring demes and the forts of Parnes") is discussed in *Supplementum Epigraphicum Graecum* (SEG) LIV (2008) no. 14.

(Sommerstein & Fletcher eds. 2007 is a recent collection with associated online database devoted to the study of the phenomenon of the oath, *horkos*, in general in the ancient, mainly Greek world: see further under section IV Religion, below.)

AUTHENTICITY

In 1972 the distinguished Oxford ancient historian Russell Meiggs finally brought out his massive, epigraphically informed treatment of the Athenian empire of the fifth century BCE (Meiggs 1972). In an important Appendix he also discussed, penetratingly, "Some controversial documents" (504–18). These included our Acharnae text (504–7, with Add. 597), which he considered "almost certainly a fabrication" (156).

Scholarship on the authenticity of the transcribed Oath was coincidentally and significantly renewed in that same year by Peter Siewert, in a book in German based on his 1970 Munich thesis (1972, cf. Siewert 1977 on the Ephebic Oath, both on and elsewhere than on the Acharnae stele). Siewert, implausibly to my mind, is for the text's original authenticity.

The elderly Louis Robert (in a review in his famous *Bulletin Épigraphique*, a supplement to *Revue des Études Grecques*, for 1973) re-articulated, specifically against Siewert, his original, sceptical line of 35 years earlier; and that is, I believe, the majority view still today, as represented for example in the latest edition of the document known to me: Rhodes & Osborne 2003: no. 88. But there are highly reputable scholars who share Siewert's view, most notably van Wees 2006, who argues that behind the Athenian or Athenian-inspired versions of the Oath lies an authentic—Spartan—original, an oath sworn regularly back home in Sparta (and not only exceptionally in a foreign context such as that of the Plataea battle) by the Spartans'"sworn bands" (131). An awful lot of heft, however, far too much, as it seems to me, is supposed to be wielded by the use in the Acharnae epigraphic text of the one certain piece of Spartan technical terminology, "enomotarch"— captain of a platoon (enômotia, literally an "under-oath entity"). The attempt by Krentz 2007 to show that behind the Acharnae stele text lies ultimately a real, authentic oath that was sworn before the battle, not of Plataea, but of Marathon, is, for all its imaginative ingenuity, also excessively speculative if not fanciful; but it fails to convince (me) principally because it does not take the fourth-century BCE ideological-commemorative context sufficiently into account.

For, much the most important, Rhodes & Osborne were able to raise the authenticity question in a new way, one that even Siewert significantly had not followed: that is, as an issue of collective cultural-historical memory. This is also the line taken in Jung 2006 (rev. by A. Petrovic *Journal of Hellenic Studies* 2009: 197–99, and by J. Dayton, *Bryn Mawr Classical Review* 2006.11.24), and the one that my book is primarily concerned to address and to explore still further. In short, I have concluded, ultimately, that the Oath of Plataea—in whatever form—is properly to be included and interpreted among a whole series of post–Persian Wars texts and documents, which commences round about 380 BCE and the authenticity of which has been intensively reexamined (e.g., by Bertrand 2005) in the light of the so-called Themistocles Decree discovered at Troezen in the 1950s by Michael Jameson, and published by him in the 1960s (Meiggs & Lewis 1969/1988: no. 23). If most of these are *certainly* inauthentic, at least in part, this makes the authenticity of the Oath of Plataea all the harder, if not impossible, to sustain. Can documents lie? They can indeed, and do: Habicht's "falsche Urkunden" ("false" or "fake" documents: Habicht 1961) gets it right.

II. Secondary Sources

PERSIA

The ancient Achaemenid Persian empire (c. 550–330 BCE) is a sensitive subject, even or perhaps especially today: Farrokh 2008. Curtis & Tallis 2005 rather surprisingly described it as a "forgotten" empire, when labeling an excellent British Museum exhibition and catalogue devoted to it, despite the facts that the "Cyrus Cylinder," a key document of the empire's founder, Cyrus II, now in the B.M.'s own collection, is transcribed honorifically in no less august and visited a space than the United Nations building in New York, and that Cyrus is mentioned *honoris causa* in the Hebrew Bible and Christian Old Testament no fewer than twenty-three times. It was not at all surprising, however, that, when in 2010 the B.M. delayed carrying out an agreed loan of the Cylinder to Iran, this caused an international diplomatic incident.

The major problem in studying and trying to do justice to the Persian empire is the lack of written materials of an objectively historical kind. Crudely, there is no Persian Herodotus or Thucydides, or even Xenophon. This tends to provoke Persian specialists either into overly defensive attempts to decry or at least deflate the claims of (above all others) Herodotus as a historian of Persia or alternatively into advancing overly laudatory claims on the empire's behalf. For the former take, see Kuhrt 2007–10, which, despite the author's slant, is an absolutely indispensable collection of Persian and Greek and other sources, brilliantly organized and annotated (sources for the Greek campaign, ending with Mycale, are on pp. 250–85; for Plataea, pp. 279–84). The latter sort of take is exemplified by Castriota 2000, who seems much keener on Persian than Athenian imperialism, and believes in the justice of Xerxes; by Wiesehöfer 2009 (a hymn to Achaemenid toleration); and by Ball 2010, who believes ancient Persia was the first to grope towards a "one-world" idea. It is quite a different matter, however, to argue, as does Holland 2005, that the Achaemenids' was the first truly "world" empire, and that the Persians were by no means as imperialist, at least in forcible imposition of an alien ideology, as some other oriental and other empires have been, before and since. Different again—indeed, flatly contradictory—is the hostile account in Lincoln 2007, with a chapter entitled "The Dark Side of Paradise" (on which concept, see below). For a discussion of official Persian Zoroastrianism, see Boyce 1975, 1982, 1994; for a long-run, ancient-modern perspective, see Rose 2011 (chapter II is on the Achaemenids). For an insight into how the Persians saw "Greece" and "Greeks," see Kuhrt 2002.

The once standard, chronologically ordered account of the Achaemenids is Olmstead 1948 (battle of Plataea at pp. 257–59), but this has now been superseded entirely both in documentation (Kuhrt 2007–2010, above) and in interpretation by Wiesehöfer 2001 and Briant 2002, among others. See also now Harrison 2011 (ch. 2 is entitled "The Persian version") for a brilliant short appreciation of the revolution in ancient Persian historical studies over the past thirty years or so, pioneered by Amélie Kuhrt and the sadly late Dutch scholar, Heleen Sancisi-Weerdenburg. Brosius 2006 is a very useful introduction (note especially the Excursus, pp. 76–78, entitled "The Creation of The Other: The Persians and the Greek-Persian Wars," in which she claims provocatively that "what truly turned Marathon, Salamis and Plataea into world-historical events was the philosophy and historiography of the nineteenth and twentieth centuries," beginning with Hegel). Also extremely helpful is Allen 2005, who observes moderately that "The events in the reigns of Darius and Xerxes forged a new identity for Persian imperial rule" (p. 57) and rather less temperately, like Kuhrt, that "a continuing stability and productivity during Xerxes' reign" conflict with Herodotus' "dynastic soap opera" (ibid.; cf. p. 83). For a brief survey, from the military point of view, see Briant 1999; at greater length, Farrokh 2007.

It is to the Persians that we owe the name if not exactly the notion of "Paradise": Allen 2005: 72 (Old Persian *paradayadam* and Avestan *pairidaeza* produced Greek *paradeisos*). That is just one of the influences that traveled West from Persia as others traveled in the opposite direction, all brilliantly tracked and discussed in Boardman 2000. For Achaemenid art, on which we are much better informed, see also Frankfort 1970: 333–78; and, through the lens of the composite "Oxus Treasure" (also now in the B.M.), Curtis 2012.

GREECE

It would not be possible to write any sort of properly historical account of the Graeco-Persian Wars without Herodotus; that is one reason why Tom Holland and I are preparing a brand-new, annotated translation for the Penguin Press (forthcoming, it is expected, in 2013). There is a ton of specialist scholarship on Herodotus, as may be seen from the recently translated Commentary on the first four Books by a formidable Italian team: Asheri et al. 2007. Marozzi 2008 is a gentler but possibly even more stimulating introduction and vade mecum to "the man who invented history." Specifically on Herodotus on Plataea, see Nyland 1992 (at pp. 93–95 he argues that his sources included medizing Greeks who fought with the Persians).

Peter Green (1996: 289n.4) has commented on Herodotus's literary skill: "just how vast and well-organised a canvas . . . how masterfully architectonic his overall aim." Pelling 2007: 149–50 makes this telling comment on his apparent lack of bias as between (loyalist) Greeks and Persians: "By the end of book 9 we may . . . be wondering how different Greeks and Persians really are. . . ." But it is necessary at the same time to keep perspective and balance. His shortcomings as a military historian are palpable, and that does not exclude his account of the Plataea battle, on which see the next section.

On the other hand, it is not necessary to be excessively sensitive to the distorting effect of Herodotus's celebration of Greek victories, as is Kuhrt, who for example counts it against him that there was "no disruption in production or major building activities throughout Xerxes' reign" (2007: 238–39). As early as 1963 Frye (1963: 147) was rightly resisting what he even then considered the "fashion" of downplaying the significance of the Persian defeats at Marathon, Salamis, and Plataia—which entailed the loss of all Darius' European conquests, a serious challenge to Persian hegemony in Western Asia, and, above all, a loss of prestige throughout the empire.

Most ancient Greek writers, including Herodotus, bought the "Athenian" line on the preeminent importance of Salamis. But one ancient Greek who did in my view correctly estimate the significance of Plataea within the context of the Graeco-Persian Wars as a whole is one of whom normally I would advise students of history to be very wary indeed—Plato! In his last dialogue, *Laws* (707), the Athenian Stranger (a surrogate for Plato himself) observes that it was Marathon and Plataea that saved Greece, not Salamis . . . ; Marathon first got the Greeks out of danger, but it was Plataea that "finally made them really safe." Cawkwell 2005 offers a useful conspectus of the post-Herodotean Greek sources on Persia's "failure."

III. The Battle Itself

Oddly enough, the (as ever anonymous) Wikipedia article on the Battle (last modified to my knowledge on July 15, 2012) is rather good. This article deals, as I have done more briefly, with the background, prelude, size, and composition of the opposing forces, strategic and tactical considerations, the battle itself, aftermath, significance, and legacy. It is relatively weak, however, both historiographically and bibliographically. It overlooks what I take to be the proper scholarly starting point—Flower & Marincola's commentary (2002) on the relevant chapters of Herodotus' *Histories* Book IX. The only "alternative" to Herodotus' account, which has its flaws (to put it mildly), is the at best third-hand narrative in Diodorus' first-century BCE "Library of History," a summary compilation lacking the qualities of Herodotus' basically investigative and critical approach. Its merits are, however, stoutly defended by Green 2006. Bibliographically, the Wikipedia article founds itself on just two modern reconstructions: that in Lazenby 1993, a scholarly military history (for this author the victory was something of a miracle), and that in Holland 2005 (344–53), a much more popular and general account aimed at a different audience (one more like Herodotus', actually). Peter Green's alternative reconstruction (1996: 264–71; cf. p. xix with 262, 236, 248, 249–50, 256, 273, 274, 281) is based on autopsy—and on a greater willingness to credit fourth-century BCE and later sources than I would myself sanction. The most recent scholarly accounts known to me include Corvisier 2011and Rusch 2011: 55–66, both very good indeed. Less convincing is Konijnendijk 2012, who argues that the Greek victory was due to a combination of logistics, luck, and sheer determination—not (*pace* Herodotus) to any technological superiority. Aimed at the general reader with a special interest in military history, Shepherd 2012 is nevertheless based in scholarship and highly recommended.

One would not normally expect to recommend a modern historical novel as a source-reference for an ancient battle, but the description in Nicholas Snow's *The Shield* (2005: 335–91, esp. 367–90), based as it is on careful autopsy of the ground, is remarkably good, and it is from this (p. 382) that I have borrowed the apt "dance of death" metaphor. (In another life Nicholas Snow is Nikolaos Kyriazis, a Professor of Economics at the University of Thessaly, Volos).

Other accounts of the battle in chronological order of publication include: Hunt 1890; Woodhouse 1898; Grundy 1901; Clark 1917; Bradford 1980 (despite its title, this deals also with 479, relevantly in chapters 27–28), for whom the Greeks' superior military technology was decisive; Burn 1962/1984: esp. ch. XXIV (pp. 509–46, with a map on p. 518 based on Grundy 1901, showing probable lines of ancient routes; at 542 n.80 he pours scorn on Diodorus-Ephorus' "conventional battle-piece in Ephoros' worst literary manner"); Pritchett 1957, 1965: ch. 8; Barron 1988; Sekunda 1992 (in a general, very well illustrated survey of the Persian army from 560 to 330 BCE); and Connolly 2012: 29–36. Never to be overlooked is any work by George

Cawkwell, whose judgment on the implications of Mardonius' failure for the history of the Persian empire I have quoted in my main text; see further on the battle Cawkwell 2005 (112–15; cf. 99, 103, 112, 214 n.3, 251–52)—he rightly emphasizes food-supply problems and morale issues, but I believe he goes too far in asserting that, from Mardonius' point of view, it was a "needless battle."

Two further sidelights: Hunt 1997 (on the role of the Spartans' Helots); and Petropoulou 2008 (death of the Persian cavalry commander Masistius and the mourning for him).

For a Persian naval perspective, see Wallinga 2005. On Salamis specifically, see most recently Shepherd & Dennis 2010, though Strauss 2004 remains the best account of Salamis known to me, even if to call it "the naval encounter that saved Greece—and Western civilization" is perhaps a little excessive. In the actual text (p. 240) Strauss concedes that Salamis was Gettysburg and Stalingrad, not Appomattox or Berlin, and that "In the end, only a wall of Spartan spears and a sea of Spartan blood would drive [the Persians] out."

IV. Religion, Greek and Athenian

The Acharnae stele is formally as well as substantively a monument of Athenian religion. Yet few scholars, not even Rhodes and Osborne, give anything like as much weight as I have (see chapter 3) to teasing out the document's many religious implications—whatever one thinks of the "authenticity question." On Athenian religion generally, see the two exemplary studies of Robert Parker: Parker 1995, 2005; together with his earlier study of pollution in the Greek world generally: Parker 1983; and now his latest study of Greek religion generally: Parker 2011. I was privileged to translate and edit what I think is still probably the best introductory textbook on ancient Greek religion: Bruit & Schmitt 1992 (and updated reprints). On Acharnae as a deme (one of the 139 or 140 villages, wards, or parishes that were the bedrock of the political geography of the Athenian democratic *polis*), see Whitehead 1985: index p. 475, s.v. "Acharnai," esp. 207 and n. 185 ("I know of no other Ares cult in a deme"); 362 (under Roman emperor Augustus, d. CE 14, the Temple of Ares was moved bodily to the Agora of Athens and reconstructed there— Spawforth 2012: 66; in 2 BCE Augustus had dedicated a famous temple to Ares' Roman equivalent, Mars, at Rome: Spawforth 2012: 66 n. 38); and App.

5 (397–400). The related deme decree of Acharnae (*Supplementum Epigraphicum Graecum* xxi.519): Whitehead 1985, Index, p. 473. On religion in the Attic demes generally, Mikalson 1977.

So far as the study of oaths in particular is concerned, Hoffmann 2005 is a good brief dictionary article, which quotes the Ephebes' Oath; he rather nicely characterizes the oath-swearer as placing himself "at the centre of the social and cosmic order with which the gods were solidary." Lateiner 2012 is a useful conspectus of oaths and practices of oath-taking, non-Greek as well as Greek, in both Herodotus and Thucydides. At greater length, on curses, see Eidinow 2007. For oaths in Homer, the Greeks' foundational author, see Kitts 2005 (those who violate oaths are doomed to suffer the same punishments as those who violate bonds of friendship and family). Plescia 1970 is an older general study; cf. Karavites 1982 (with special reference to treaty-making). We are fortunate now in that Alan Sommerstein has recently been the Principal Investigator for a wide-ranging project on ancient oath-taking based at Nottingham University in the UK. His first collective publication (Sommerstein & Fletcher eds 2007) unfortunately does rather minimize our Oath (there is a small image of the Acharnae stele on the cover but barely a notice of its texts inside), but the contributors between them discuss intelligently a wide range of representative examples, many of them taken from Athenian history. There is also, as an outcome of the project, a new online database of the oath in Archaic and Classical Greece:

http://www.nottingham.ac.uk/classics/oaths/database/index.php.

The Acharnae document is there classified as ID 338.

For political oaths, see esp. Rhodes 2007. That Aristophanes gives a comic parody of a political oath in his *Ecclesiazusae* of c. 392 (lines 41–45) indicates their serious importance in real Athenian life. Other discussions of oaths at Athens include Mirhady 1991 and Herman 2007: at p. 141. Outside Athens one might draw special attention to the oath (*horkion, horkia*) attributed probably anachronistically to the original founders of Cyrene in c. 630 (Meiggs & Lewis 1969/1988: no. 5); this too includes curses (*arai*), as likewise does a Sacred Law from Chios of c. 335 BC, where the curses are deemed to afflict the offenders preemptively. Spartans were supposed to be rigidly pious, so when a Spartan was unconventional, he was likely to be—or thought to be—a perjurer: King Cleomenes I (in 494, against the Argives) and Lysander, of set purpose at all times ("one tricks boys with knucklebones, men with oaths": Plutarch *Life of Lysander* 8.5, *Moralia* 229B (4)), both fitted that bill.

FURTHER READING

177

V. Commemorations

Holland 2010 is a recent study of propaganda issued during the Graeco-Persian Wars. Barron 1988: 619–20 offers a brief conspectus of post-War commemorations. Jung 2006 focuses specifically on Marathon and Plataea as "sites of memory." Pritchard ed. 2011 is an outstanding collection of essays on war, democracy, and culture in Classical Athens. Low 2003 considers forms of commemoration of war in fifth-century Greece outside Athens; Day 2010 concentrates on epigrams and dedications down to the early fifth century. Scott 2010 is a comprehensive account of the "spatial politics" of commemoration at the two major Panhellenic sanctuaries of Delphi and Olympia. For the "Serpent Column" commemoration of the Battle of Plataea at Delphi, placed in the widest context of "art as plunder," see Miles 2008: 39 and fig. 5. On ancient Greek "panhellenism," an ideal to which lip service was more often paid than proper respect, it often seems, see also Mitchell 2007.

On Simonides, especially the "new" Simonides, see Boedeker & Sider eds. 2001, which includes Shaw 2001 (on the possible place of performance); note also Kowerski 2003.

On the Athenian *Epitaphios* (sc. Logos) or Funeral Oration, see the marvelously original monograph of Loraux 1986.

Spawforth 2012 is a splendid, original account of the place of Greece within what the author calls "the Augustan cultural revolution"; in a chapter that "has tried to show that the reign of Augustus marked a decisive new stage in the long-standing Greek tradition of commemorating the Persian Wars" (p. 138) a special section is devoted to Plataea (130–38), which adds significantly to the perception already registered by Alcock (2002: 80) that an "incredibly dense network of ritual activity" had evolved there over the centuries from the Classical Greek to the Roman Imperial era.

On Constantine's Hippodrome in Constantinople (formerly Byzantion, later Istanbul), site of the relocated "Serpent Column," see now Eastmond 2012 (with evocative illustrations of the Ottoman-period as well late Antique Hippodrome). On Byzantion-Constantinople, see further Cartledge 2011: chapter 12.

Bridges et al. eds. 2007 is a splendid compilation of studies of cultural responses to the Wars down to our own day. Therein McGregor-Morris 2007: 235

n.11, exploring the post-mediaeval rediscovery of the Persian War battlefields, sadly notes that "since the Middle Ages, Plataea has been regarded as the least significant of the major encounters of the Persian Wars." Wrongly so! The epigraphic "Oath of Plataea" and the monument of which it forms an integral part are not exactly—and not entirely—a "war-memorial," but there is nevertheless much to be gained from a comparative reading of Reinhard Koselleck's "War memorials: identity formations of the survivors," in Koselleck 2002: 285–326.

VI. Clash of Civilizations?

Thompson 1921 is a clear statement of the once standard triumphalist view of "East is East and West is West"—and We are West and They are East: "it would be strange ingratitude on our part to forget that it was this very urgency for the sane, for the rational, which ensured that our civilization was founded on hard realistic thinking, and not on a mere drift of emotionality" (pp. 157–58). More unusually, the Cambridge scholar T. R. Glover (1917: 198) had attempted to strike a balance between East and West: "Persia has contributed to the progress of mankind both by what she has done and by what she failed to do." Said 1978/1995 is the classic modern riposte to what he identified as "orientalism" in a pejorative sense. Farrokh 2008 (accessed 03/09/2009) likewise decries what he calls "nordicism" (a version of "orientalism"). The debate continues, taking various more and less scholarly forms.

Harrison, T. ed. 2002 is a very useful collection of reprinted essays; in his general introduction the editor rightly notes (p. 4) that "The Persian Wars organized such stereotypes of the east, sharpening the focus, for example, of the contrasts between eastern luxury and Greek simplicity, despotism and democracy, and emphasizing (if not initiating) an assumption of Greek superiority." Included in the Harrison collection is one of the very best essays on what its author calls "The problem of Greek nationality": Walbank 1951/2002; Walbank uses the citizen-state of Plataea as an illustration of "the vigour with which the member of the *polis* maintained his own political identity"—as a citizen-member of Plataea, note, not of "Greece." Tom Holland plays a variation on a theme by Benedetto Croce, that all history is contemporary history: "The Persian Wars may be ancient history, but they are also . . . contemporary history, too"—and in a new and urgent way since 2001 (2005: xxii–xxiii). Adib-Moghaddam 2010 somehow thinks there was not ever a clash of civilizations, but that seems wildly over-optimistic—and is a view taken not from an ancient but a post-Islam(ist) perspective. Other relevant works are cited in the main chapter text above.

Bibliography

Adib-Moghaddam, A. *A Metahistory of the Clash of Civilisations: Us and Them beyond Orientalism.* London, 2010.

Alcock, S. E. *Archaeologies of the Greek Past: Landscape, Monuments and Memories.* Cambridge, 2002.

Allen, L. *The Persian Empire: A History.* London, 2005.

Ball, Warwick. *Towards One World: Ancient Persia and the West.* London, 2010.

Barron, J. P. "The Liberation of Greece." In *Cambridge Ancient History.* 2nd ed. Vol. IV, *Persia, Greece and the Western Mediterranean c. 525–479 B.C.,* 592–622. Cambridge, 1988.

Bertrand, J-M. "Inscriptions dites fausses et histoire, en Grèce ancienne." *Revista De Historiografia* 3, II (2005): 78–85.

Boardman, J. *Persia and the West: An Archaeological Investigation of the Genesis of Achaemenid Art.* London, 2000.

Boedeker, D. "The View from Eleusis. Demeter in the Persian Wars." In Bridges et al., eds., *Cultural Responses to the Persian Wars,* 65–82.

Boedeker, D., and D. Sider, eds. *The New Simonides: Contexts of Praise and Desire.* New York and Oxford, 2001.

Boyce, M. *History of Zoroastrianism.* 3 vols. Leiden, 1975, 1982, 1994.

Bradford, E. *The Year of Thermopylae.* London, 1980.

Briant, P. "The Achaemenid Empire." In K. Raaflaub and N. Rosenstein, eds., *War and Society in the Ancient and Medieval Worlds: Asia, the Mediterranean, Europe, and Mesoamerica,* 105–28. Washington, D.C., 1999.

———. *From Cyrus to Alexander: A History of the Persian Empire.* Winona Lake, Ind., 2002.

Bridges, E., E. Hall, and P. Rhodes, eds. *Cultural Responses to the Persian Wars: Antiquity to the Third Millennium.* Oxford, 2007.

Brosius, M. *The Persian Empire from Cyrus II to Artaxerxes I.* London, 2000.

———. *The Persians: An Introduction.* London and New York, 2006.

Bruit Zaidman, L., and P. Schmitt Pantel. *Religion in the Ancient Greek City.* Translated and edited by P. Cartledge. Cambridge, 1992.

Bulwer Lytton, E. *Athens: Its Rise and Fall.* Edited by O. Murray. London and New York, 1837/2004.

Burn, A. R. *Persia and the Greek: The Defence of the West, 546–478 B.C.* London, 1962/1984.

Carson, A. *Economy of the Unlost: Reading Simonides of Keos with Paul Celan.* Princeton, 1999.

Cartledge, P. A. *The Greeks: A Portrait of Self and Others.* 2nd ed. Oxford, 2002.

———. *Ancient Greek Political Thought in Practice.* Cambridge, 2009.

———. *Ancient Greece: A Very Short Introduction.* Oxford, 2011.

Castriota, D. "Justice, Kingship and Imperialism: Rhetoric and Reality in Fifth-century B.C. Representations Following the Persian Wars." In B. Cohen, ed., *Not the Classical Ideal: Athens and the Construction of the Other in Greek Art,* 443–79. Leiden, 2000.

Cawkwell, G. *The Greek War: The Failure of Persia.* Oxford, 2005.

Clark, R. T. "The Campaign of Plataiai." *Classical Philology* 12, no. 1 (1917): 30–48.

Connolly, P. *Greece and Rome at War.* Barnsley, 2012 [originally 1981, rev. 1998].

Corvisier, J-N. *La bataille de Platées, 479 av. J-C.* Paris, 2011.

Curtis, J. *The Oxus Treasure.* "British Museum Objects in Focus" series. London, 2012.

Curtis, J., and N. Tallis, eds. *A Forgotten Empire: The World of Ancient Persia.* London, 2005.

Daux, G. "Deux stèles d'Acharne." In *Kharisterion eis Anastasion K. Orlandon.* Vol. I, 78–90. Athens, 1965.

Day, J. W. *Archaic Greek Epigram and Dedication: Representation and Reperformance.* Cambridge, 2010.

Dillery, J. "Reconfiguring the Past: Thyrea, Thermopylae and Narrative Patterns in Herodotus." *American Journal of Philology* 117, no. 2 (1996): 217–54.

Eastmond, A. "The Hippodrome of Constantinople and the Last Chariot Race." In J. J. Kierkuc-Bielinski and G. John, eds., *Stadia: Sport and Vision in Architecture*, 48–57. London (Sir John Soane's Museum), 2012.

Eidinow, E. *Oracles, Curses and Risk among the Ancient Greeks.* Oxford, 2007.

Elliott, J. *Mirrors of the Unseen: Journeys in Iran.* London, 2006.

Farrokh, K. *Shadows in the Desert: Ancient Persia at War.* Oxford, 2007.

———. "Response to Spiegel's attack on the legacy of Cyrus the Great." http://www.kavehfarrokh.com/articles/nordicism/response-to-spiegel-magazine-2/, 2008. First accessed 3/9/2009.

Fisher, D. *Morality and War: Can War Be Just in the Twenty-first Century?* Oxford, 2011.

Flower, M., and J. Marincola (ed. and comm.). *Herodotus The Histories, Book IX.* Cambridge, 2002.

Frankfort, H. *The Art and Architecture of the Ancient Orient.* 4th rev. impr. Harmondsworth, 1970.

Frontisi-Ducroux, F., and F. Lissarrague. "Signe, objet, support: regard privé, regard public." In F. de Polignac and P. Schmitt, eds., *Public et privé en Grèce ancienne*, 135–47. Paris, 1998. (= *Ktèma* 23: 137–44.)

Frye, R. N. *The Heritage of Persia.* New York and Toronto, 1963.

Gagné, R. "What Is the Pride of Halicarnassus?" *Classical Antiquity* 25, no. 1 (2006): 1–33.

Glover, T. R. "Persia." In *From Pericles to Philip*, 197–234. London, 1917.

Grayling, A. C. *The Good Book: A Secular Bible.* Walsall, 2011 [to be reissued in paperback in 2013 as *The Good Book: A Humanist Bible*].

Green, P. *The Greco-Persian Wars.* Berkeley, 1996.

Green, P. *Diodorus Siculus Books 11–12.37.1: Greek History, 480–431 BC—the Alternative Version.* Austin, Tex., 2006.

Grundy, G. B. *The Great Persian War and Its Preliminaries.* London, 1901.

Habicht, C. "Falsche Urkunden zur Geschichte Athens im Zeitalter der Perserkriege." *Hermes* 89 (1961): 1–35.

Harrison, T., ed. *Greeks and Barbarians.* Edinburgh, 2002.

———. *Writing Ancient Persia.* London, 2011.

Hedrick, C.W. Jr. "The American Ephebe: The Ephebic Oath, U.S. Education, and Nationalism." *Classical World* 97 (2004): 385–407.

Herman, G. "Rituals of Evasion in Ancient Greece." In G. Herman and I. Shatzman, eds., *Greeks Between East and West: Essays in Greek History and Literature in Memory of David Asheri*, 136–59. Jerusalem, 2007.

Hoffmann, G. "Serment (Grèce)." In J. Leclant, ed., *Dictionnaire de l'Antiquité*. Paris, 2005.

Holland, T. *Persian Fire: The First World Empire and the Battle for the West.* London, 2005.

———. "From Persia with Love: Propaganda and Imperial Over-reach in the Greco-Persian Wars." In V. D. Hanson, ed., *Makers of Ancient Strategy*, 11–30. Princeton, 2010.

Hornblower, S. "Thucydides and Plataian Perjury." In Sommerstein and Fletcher, eds., *HORKOS: The Oath in Greek Society*, 138–47.

Hunt, P. "Helots at the Battle of Plataea." *Historia* 46, no. 2 (1997): 129–44.

Hunt, W. Irving "Discoveries at Plataia in 1890. IV. Notes on the Battlefield of Plataia." *American Journal of Archeology* 6, no. 4 (1890): 463–75.

Jung, M. *Marathon und Plataia: Zwei Perserschlachten als "lieux de mémoire" im antiken Griechenland*. Göttingen, 2006.

Karavites, P. *Promise-giving and Treaty-making*. Leiden, 1982.

Kellogg, D. "The Attic Deme of Acharnai: History and Identity." Unpublished Ph.D. diss., University of Pennsylvania, 2005.

———. "The Ephebic Oath and the Oath of Plataia in Fourth-Century Athens." *Mouseion*, 3rd ser., 8 (2008): 355–76.

Kitts, M. *Sanctified Violence in Homeric Society: Oath-Making Rituals and Narratives in the* Iliad. Cambridge, 2005.

Konijnendijk, N. "'Neither the less valorous nor the weaker': Persian Military Might and the Battle of Plataea." *Historia* 61 (2012): 1–17.

Koselleck, R. *The Practice of Conceptual History: Timing History, Spacing Concepts*. Stanford, Calif., 2002.

Kowerski, L. M. "Simonides on the Persian Wars: A Study of the Elegiac Verses of the 'New Simonides.'" Ph.D. diss., Rutgers University, 2003.

Krentz, P. M. "The Oath of Marathon, not Plataea." *Hesperia* 76 (2007): 731–42.

Kuhrt, A. "*Greeks*" and "*Greece*" in Mesopotamian and Persian Perspectives (J. L. Myres Memorial Lecture 21). Oxford, 2002.

————. *The Persian Empire*. 2 vols. London and New York, 2007 [repr. in 1 vol. 2010].

Lane Fox, R. *The Classical World*. London, 2006.

Lateiner, D. "Oaths: Theory and Practice in the Histories of Herodotus and Thucydides." In E. Foster and D. Lateiner, eds., *Thucydides and Herodotus*, 154–84. Oxford, 2012.

Lawton, C. L. *Attic Document Reliefs: Art and Politics in Ancient Athens*. Oxford, 1995.

Lazenby, J. F. *The Spartan Army*. Warminster, 1985.

————. *The Defence of Greece*. Warminster, 1993.

Lewis, J. D. *Nothing Less Than Victory: Decisive Wars and the Lessons of History*. Princeton, 2010.

Lincoln, B. *Religion, Empire, and Torture: The Case of Achaemenian Persia, with a Postscript on Abu Ghraib*. Chicago, 2007.

Loraux, N. *The Invention of Athens. The Funeral Oration in the Classical City*. Boston, 1981/1986.

Low, P. A. "Remembering War in Fifth-century Greece: Ideologies, Societies, and Commemoration beyond Democratic Athens." *World Archaeology* 35 (2003): 98–111.

Mackenzie, Compton. *Marathon and Salamis. The Battles That Defined the Western World*. Yardley, Penn., 1934 (repr. 2010).

Marincola, J. "The Persian Wars in Fourth-Century Oratory and Historiography." In Bridges et al., eds., 105–25.

————. "Plutarch, 'Parallelism' and the Persian-War *Lives*." In N. Humble, ed., *Plutarch's Lives: Parallelism and Purpose*, 121–43. Swansea, 2010.

Marozzi, J. *The Man Who Invented History: Travels with Herodotus*. London, 2007.

McGregor-Morris, I. "'Shrines of the Mighty': Rediscovering the Battlefields of the Persian Wars." In Bridges et al., eds., 231–64.

Meiggs, R. *The Athenian Empire*. Oxford, 1972.

Meiggs, R., and D. M. Lewis. *A Selection of Greek Historical Inscriptions*. Oxford, 1969/1988.

Mikalson, J. D. "Religion in the Attic Demes." *American Journal of Philology* 98 (1977): 424–35.

Miles, M. M. *Art as Plunder: The Ancient Origins of Debate about Cultural Property*. Cambridge, 2008.

Mirhady, D. "The Oath-challenge in Athens." *Classical Quarterly* 41, no. 1 (1991): 78–83.

Mitchell, L. *Panhellenism and the Barbarian in Archaic and Classical Greece.* Swansea, 2007.

Nyland, R. "Herodotos' Sources for the Plataiai Campaign." *L'Antiquité Classique* 61 (1992): 80–97.

Ober, J. *Fortress Attica: Defense of the Athenian Land Frontier 404–322 B.C.* Leiden, 1985.

Olmstead, A. T. *History of the Persian Empire.* Chicago, 1948.

Pagden, A. *Worlds at War: The 2,500-Year Struggle between East and West.* Oxford, 2008.

Parker, R. C. T. *Miasma: Pollution and Purification in Early Greek Religion.* Oxford, 1983.

———. *Athenian Religion: A History.* Oxford, 1996.

———. *Polytheism and Society at Athens.* Oxford, 2005.

———. *On Greek Religion.* Ithaca, N.Y., 2011.

Pelling, C. "De Malignitate Plutarchi: Plutarch, Herodotus, and the Persian Wars." In Bridges et al., eds., 145–64.

Petropoulou, A. "The Death of Masistios and the Mourning for His Loss (Hdt. 9.20–25.1)." In S. M. Reza Darbandi and A. Zournatzi, eds., *Ancient Greece and Ancient Iran. Cross-cultural Encounters* (Athens, November 11–13, 2006), 9–30. Athens, 2008.

Platonos-Yiota, M. *Akharnai. Istoriki kai topographiki episkopisi tôn arkhaiôn Akharnôn, tôn yeitonikôn dimôn kai tôn okhurôseôn tis Parnithas.* Acharnae, 2004 [in Greek].

Plescia, J. *The Oath and Perjury in Ancient Greece.* Tallahassee, Fla., 1970.

Prakken, D. W. "Note on the Apocryphal Oath of the Athenians at Plataea." *American Journal of Philology* 61 (1940): 62–65.

Pritchard, D., ed. *War, Democracy and Culture in Classical Athens.* Cambridge, 2011.

Pritchett, W. K. "New Light on Plataia." *American Journal of Archaeology* 61 (1957): 9–28.

———. *Studies in Ancient Greek Topography.* Vol. I. Berkeley, 1965.

Rhodes, P. J. "Oaths in Political Life." In Sommerstein and Fletcher, eds., 11–25. Exeter, 2007.

Rhodes, P. J., and R. Osborne. *Greek Historical Inscriptions 404–323 BC.* Oxford, 2003.

Robert, L. *Etudes épigraphiques et philologiques*. Paris, 1938.

————. "Bulletin épigraphique" (supplement to *Revue des Etudes Grecques* 86 [1973]) [a review of Siewert 1972].

Rose, J. *Zoroastrianism: An Introduction*. London and New York, 2011.

Rusch, S. *Sparta at War: Strategy, Tactics and Campaigns 550–362 BC*. London, 2011.

Said, Edward. *Orientalism*. New edition with Afterword. London, 1978/1995.

Scott, M. *Delphi and Olympia: The Spatial Politics of Panhellenism in the Archaic and Classical Periods*. Cambridge, 2010.

Sebillotte Cuchet, V. *Libérez la patrie! Patriotisme et politique en Grèce ancienne*. Paris, 2006.

Sebillotte Cuchet, V. "Une politique des genres, le serment des éphèbes athéniens." In V. Sebillotte Cuchet and N. Ernout, eds., *Problèmes du Genre en Grèce ancienne*, 233–45. St-Just-La-Pendue, 2007.

Sekunda, N. *The Persian Army 560–330 BC*. Oxford and New York, 1992.

Shaw, P-J. "Lords of Hellas, Old Men of the Sea: The Occasion of Simonides' Elegy." In Boedeker and Sider, eds., 164–81.

Shear, J. *Polis and Revolution. Responding to Oligarchy in Classical Athens*. Cambridge, 2011.

Shepherd, W. *Salamis* (Osprey). Illustrated by Peter Dennis. Botley and Long Island City, N.Y., 2010.

————. *Plataea 479 BC: The Most Glorious Victory Ever Seen* (Osprey). Illustrated by Peter Dennis. Botley and Long Island City, N.Y., 2012.

Siewert, P. *Der Eid von Plataiai* (Vestigia 16). Munich, 1972.

————. "The Ephebic Oath in Fifth-century Athens." *Journal of Hellenic Studies* 97 (1977): 102–11.

Snow, N. [N. Kyriazis]. *The Shield*. Bloomington, Ind., 2005.

Snow, N. *Marathon and Freedom*. Forthcoming.

Sommerstein, A. H., and J. Fletcher, eds. *HORKOS: The Oath in Greek Society*. Exeter, 2007.

Spawforth, A. J. S. *Greece and the Augustan Cultural Revolution*. Cambridge, 2012.

Steinbock, B. "A lesson in Patriotism: Lycurgus' *Against Leocrates*, the Ideology of the Ephebeia and Athenian Social Memory." *Classical Antiquity* 30 (2011): 297–317

Strauss, B. S. *Salamis: The Naval Encounter that Saved Greece—and Western Civilization*. New York, 2004 [also published as *Salamis: The Greatest Naval Battle of the Ancient World, 480 BC*. London].

Thomson, J. O. *Greeks and Barbarians*. London, 1921.

Tod, M. N. *Greek Historical Inscriptions*. Vol. II. Oxford, 1948.

Van Wees, H. "'The oath of the sworn bands': The Acharnae Stela, the Oath of Plataea and Archaic Spartan Warfare." In A. Luther, M. Meier, and L. Thommen, eds., *Das Frühe Sparta*, 125–64. Stuttgart, 2006.

Walbank, F. W. "The Problem of Greek Nationality" (1951). Repr. in Harrison, ed., 234–56.

Wallinga, H. T. *Xerxes' Greek Adventure: The Naval Perspective*. Leiden, 2005.

Walzer, M. *Just and Unjust War: A Moral Argument with Historical Illustrations*. 4th ed. New York, 2006.

Whatley, N. "On the Possibility of Reconstructing Marathon and Other Ancient Battles." *Journal of Hellenic Studies* 84 (1964): 119–39.

Whitehead, D. M. *The Demes of Attica 508/7–ca. 250 B.C.: A Political and Social Study*. Princeton, 1985.

Wiesehöfer, J. *Ancient Persia from 550 B.C. to 650 A.D.* London, 2001.

———. "The Achaemenid empire." In I. Morris and W. Scheidel, eds., *The Dynamics of Ancient Empires: State Power from Assyria to Byzantium*, 66–98. New York, 2009.

Winter, J. *Sites of Memory, Sites of Mourning*. Cambridge, 1995.

Woodhouse, W. J. "The Greeks at Plataiai." *Journal of Hellenic Studies* 18 (1898): 33–59.

Note also the following online/electronic resources:

Aerial map: http://www.panoramio.com/photo/11023855

History Channel Battle of Plataea: http://www.300spartanwarriors.com/battleofplataea.html

Index

Note: Page numbers in *italics* denote illustrations and maps.

Feuerbach, Ludwig, 166–67
First World War, 141
Foundation Charter (of Susa), 69
Fox, Robin Lane, 145
Freedom Festival, 129
French School at Athens, 6, 12
frontiers, 50–51
Funeral Speech. See *Epitaphios*

Gates of Fire (Pressfield), 165
Gelon, 136, 154
Generals, Athenian, 36, 76
Germany, 5
The Good Book: A Secular Bible
    (Grayling), 165–66
Graeco-Persian Wars
    and cultural legacy of Plataea,
        166–67
    final engagements of, 120
    and Hellenic identity, 80, 81
    and Herodotus's *Histories*, 60–64
    and legacy of Plataea, 163–64
    and oath at Corinth, 26
    and origin of Oath of Plataea, 7
    and status of Sparta, 142
    See also specific battles
Grayling, Anthony, 165–66
Great Battles (MacDonogh), xii
Great King of Persia. *See* Darius I;
    Xerxes
Great Panathenaea, 49, 50, 152
Greek forces at Battle of Plataea,
    xxii–xxiii, 8
Green, Peter, 141

Halicarnassus, 53, 60, 158
harem system, royal, 78

heavy infantry forces, 76, 79, 106,
    109–12
Hebrew Bible, 63
Hegemone, 15, 50
Helen of Troy, 143
Hellanodikai, 47
Hellas, 64, 79–87
Hellenic identity
    and Athens, 33, 79–87,
        102, 122
    and colonization, 85–86
    and democracy, 82, 124–27
    and Herodotus, 102, 109, 146
    and legacy of Plataea, 162–67
    and loyalty oaths, 17, 29–30
    and polytheism, 43
    and Sparta, 79–87
Hellenic League, 26, 28–29, 93
Hellespont (Dardanelles), 31, 65,
    91, 97
Helots
    and Battle of Plataea,
        106–7, 117
    and Greek slave systems, 82–83
    laws regarding treatment of, 52
    rebellion of, 133
    and religious curses, 52
    and Spartan citizenship, 138
    at Thermopylae, 95
Hera, 116
Heracles, 15, 50
Herodotus, *61*
    and the Achaemenid Empire,
        65, 68
    and ancestor veneration, 157–58
    on the Battle of Marathon, 74–76
    on the Battle of Mycale, 121

militarism
  and Acharnae, 35
  and Ephebes, 37–38
  and legacy of Plataea, 163
  military titles, 18, 19, 36
  and Spartan civic structure,
    38–39
Mill, John Stuart, xi
Miller, Frank, 165
Miltiades, 76, 98, 136
Mount Kithairon, 105–6
Mount Olympus, 46–47, 48
myth-making, 145–46

naval power and warfare
  and the Achaemenid Empire, 73, 79
  and Athenian democracy, 84
  and Atheno-Spartan rivalry,
    30–31
  Battle of Artemisium, 62, 88,
    97–98
  Battle of Marathon, 75
  Battle of Mycale, 120–21
  and the Ionian Revolt, 73
  and the Peace of Callias, 33–34
  See also Battle of Salamis
Nemea, 137
Nicias, 31, 33
nomads, 71

"The Oath" (2010), 43
Oath of Plataea
  and Athenian identity, 58
  authenticity of, 3–4, 7, 10, 13–14,
    28–30, 104–5
  context of, 30–39, 42–47
  dedication of, 14–15

discovery of, 6, 12
and divine authority, 44–45, 51–52
epigraphic nature of, 13, 25
purpose and function of, 4, 30, 41
sanction for violation of, 6–7
text of, 16, 26, 34
See also Battle of Plataea; Ephebic
    Oath; stele with Oath of Plataea
    inscription
oaths and oath-taking
  and Athens, 54–58
  autonomy oaths, 149
  cultural context of Oath of
    Plataea, 42–47
  Ephebic Oath, 6, 15–16, 26,
    38–39, 50, 157
  and Greek religion, 43–45
  oath of Amnesty, 57–58
  oaths of alliance, 93
  Olympic, 46–47
  and polytheism, 50
  religious significance of, 7, 9,
    51–52
  See also Oath of Plataea
Oeneus, 37
"official" histories, 63
Oineis, 37
Old Persian (language), 67
oligarchic rule, 56–57, 82, 84, 103
Olympia, 47, 133, 136–37, 161
Olympic Games, 46–47, 80,
    119–20, 162–63
omens, 113, 116
Orchomenus, 23
orientalism, 164
ostracism, 55
Oxyrhynchus, 142

INDEX

silver, 84
Simonides, 139–44
Sites of Memory, Sites of Mourning
    (Winter), 141
Skias, 132
slavery, 81–82, 83–84. *See also*
    Helots
Snow, Nicholas. *See* Kyriazis,
    Nikolaos
Socrates, 166
Solon, 54–55, 84
Sparta
    and accounts of Plataea battle,
        115
    and the Achaemenid Empire, 64
    and *The Acharnians*, 37
    arms and armor, *111*
    and Atheno-Peloponnesian
        War, 31–32
    and Battle of Marathon, 9
    and Battle of Thermopylae, 17,
        95–96
    and burial customs, 21
    casualties of Plataea, 117
    and city destruction, 23
    competition with Athens, 9
    and cooperation against
        Persians, 30
    and the Covenant of Plataea,
        127–28
    and curses, 52
    and democracy, 82
    destruction of Plataea, 159–60
    and diplomatic envoys, 101–2
    and frontier-crossing rituals, 51
    and Hellenic identity, 80–87, 122
    and the Hellenic League, 93–94

and hoplite military tactics, 85
and militarism, 38–39
military-political structure, 141
and naval warfare, 31
and obedience to authority, 19,
    118–19
and obscurity of Battle
    of Plataea, 89
and oligarchic rule, 82, 103
and origin of Oath text, 19
and public architecture, 131–35
rebellion against Macedon, 27
religiosity of, 118–19
rivalry with Athens, 9–10,
    30–31, 147
siege of Plataea, 149
and Simonides, 144
and slavery, 82–84
and text of Oath of Plataea, 17
Thucydides on, 148
and xenophobia, 150
stasis, 52–53, 54–58, 146, 149
stele with Oath of Plataea
    inscription, 2
    authenticity of, 28–30
    dedicant of, 14, 34
    and deme of Acharnae, 13–14
    discovery of, 12
    and the Ephebic Oath, 38, 39, 157
    original location, 6
    and polytheism, 43
    sculptural decorations, 34–35, 43
    and text of Oath, 16, 26, 34
subjective view of history, 59–60
Susa, 69, 71
symbols, 3
Syracuse, 86, 136